THE HARMONY OF DISSONANCE:

AGELESS CONNECTIONS

Sarah Lipton, Regina (Rifke) Krummel

Copyright © 2020 by GENUINE, Inc.
All rights reserved under International and Pan-American Copyright Conventions.

Published in the United States by GENUINE, Inc.
501c3
genuinenetwork.org

Cover designed by Crys Goure – www.crystalgoure.com
Photos used with permission by Sarah Lipton from her family's archived photos

ISBN: 978-0-5788147-8-0
December 2020
Version 1.0

DEDICATION

This book is dedicated to all who seek their heart's true home. Through all the storms of pain and loss, may we all find our way back home to *love*.

Sarah dedicates this book to her strong, bright, funny, and wonderful daughters, Odessa Rose and Indigo Poppy, and thanks her sweet husband Scott Robbins for sticking with her through all the cycles of life.

Regina dedicates this book to her wonderful, constant friend and husband William Krummel, her three children, six grandchildren, and all who wander the roads back home to themselves.

CONTENTS

Introduction 1
    First, Sarah Speaks 1
    And Now, Rifke Speaks 6

Chapter One: Let's Be Honest 10
    October 23, 2015 – Rifke 10
    October 30, 2015 – Sarah 11

Enter: The Voice of Our Story 14
    February 10, 2019 – Sarah 14

Chapter Two: The Irritation of Dissonance 16
    November 2, 2015 – Sarah 16
    December 4, 2015 – Sarah, Rifke 18
    December 2, 2015 – Sarah 21
    December 3, 2015 – Rifke 22

Chapter Three: Surviving Amongst Shards 23
    November 2, 2015 – Sarah 23
    December 3, 2015 – Rifke, Sarah 23
    December 5, 2015 – Rifke 25
    December 7, 2015 – Sarah 25
    December 10, 2015 – Rifke 28

Enter: the Voice of Mildred Zimmerman 29
    Memoirs for Sarah, A Very Long Letter 29
    A Glass of Tea 31

    The Piano 32

Chapter Four: Listening to Our Ancestors 34

    December 11, 2015 – Sarah 34

    February 8, 2019 – Sarah 34

    October 26, 2015 – Sarah 36

    April 2, 2016 – Rifke 40

    November 18, 2015 – Sarah 41

    November 19, 2015 – Rifke 42

    November 20, 2015 – Sarah 43

    November 21, 2015 – Rifke 44

Chapter Five: Red and Purple 45

    December 15, 2015 – Rifke 45

    January 18, 2016 – Sarah 46

    January 27, 2016 – Rifke 47

    January 28, 2016 – Sarah 48

    February 7, 2016 – Rifke 48

    February 8, 2016 – Sarah 49

    February 9, 2016 – Rifke 49

    February 11, 2016 – Sarah 50

    February 12, 2016 – Rifke 51

    February 18, 2016 – Sarah 52

    February 23, 2016 – Sarah 52

    February 23, 2016 – Rifke 52

    February 26, 2016 – Sarah 52

    March 2, 2016 – Rifke 53

    March 3, 2016 – Sarah 54

    March 3, 2016 – Rifke 56

    March 28, 2016 – Sarah 56

Chapter Six: Who is Behind the Woodpile? 59

April 2, 2016 – Sarah 59
April 3, 2016 – Writing Next To Each Other 60
October 20, 2017 – Rifke 65
October 24, 2017 – Sarah 66
October 24, 2017 – Rifke 67
November 7, 2017 – Sarah 68
February 2, 2018 – Rifke 69
February 5, 2018 – Sarah 70
February 6, 2018 – Rifke, Sarah 71
February 15, 2018 – Rifke 74
February 19, 2018 – Sarah 75

Chapter Seven: Accessible Darkness 76

February 28, 2018 – Writing Next To Each Other 76
March 2, 2018 – Rifke 79
March 8, 2018 – Rifke 79
March 16, 2018 – Rifke 81
March 20, 2018 – Rifke 81
April 30, 2018 – Rifke 82
March 2, 2018 – Rifke 83
June 5, 2018 – Rifke, Sarah 84

Chapter Eight: Conclusion, For Now 86

March 8, 2020 – Sarah, Rifke 86

Afterword 94

Acknowledgements 95

About the Authors 96

INTRODUCTION

The Karzinell Family, November 17, 1910, Pinsk, Russia.
Sarah Lipton and Regina Krummel's ancestors, left to right: Avraham (Sarah's great-great-grandfather), Mary (Merele: Sarah's great-grandmother), Yehudit (Judith: Sarah's great-great-grandmother), and Mary's brothers and sisters.

FIRST, SARAH SPEAKS

In the beginning, we do not necessarily know our story.

It was that way for me when I started writing with my long-lost cousin Regina (whom I call Rifke and sometimes use the Yiddish-ized endearment for: Rifkele. Rifke is a distant cousin of my late beloved grandmother Mildred (Nana to me), and is a human who, as you will see, has always seen me, even though we can't quite figure out how we're related other than to know we go back to the "Old Country."

For many years, I searched for belonging. I stridently took to the road to find myself in the world. I sank deep onto the meditation cushion to find myself. I traveled back in place, and almost, in time, to find myself amongst the reeds by my ancestral river.

And in the end, the only place I ever truly found myself was in the journey of writing this book, cousin Rifke by my side all along the way. It is through story that we meet ourselves. It is through discovering the tapestry of our ancestors that we begin to meet our inheritance. Meeting our ancestors shakes the chaff from the grain and the extraneous substance blows up and away from the rich harvest. Who we actually are is finally revealed in all our grainy glory beneath.

In living color, Regina (Rifke) Krummel and I (Sarah Lipton) have found a way to journey back to our ancestors, and, every time, it tastes like the sudden catch of sun sparking golden off a winter-green pine bough. It's the feeling of a mighty wind blowing so intently that all thoughts cease and there is only the sensation of wind.

Together we share what follows—a meandering journey of connection, of harmony, and dissonance, written between 2015 and 2020. It's not a particularly svelte journey. But we are of Russian Jewish stock, and we ourselves are not known for being svelte. We traverse numerous topics including: gut-wrenching honesty, the irritation and resolution of dissonance, the bitter joy of surviving amongst shards, the gift of listening to our ancestors, weaving colors of red and purple, making the darkness accessible, why pain is important, and asking the ancient question—who is behind the woodpile?

The dissonance is felt in the sticky, uncomfortable process of unpicking the threads of the story. How we are, how we've been seen, how we've avoided being seen, how we've been harmed along the way, these dissonant chords come up again and again. Investigating the pain actually liberates us from the pain. And when we allow ourselves to traverse that treacherous terrain, we emancipate ourselves from the stuck patterns. It turns out, when we feel and perceive the presence of our ancestors in our daily life, harmony arises. The resonance occurs because in fact: they have never left us, and when we allow their presence to warm our hearts, our life's melody is enriched, deepened, and satisfied.

We become resourced.

The willingness to do the deep dive, that's the key. There is a hunger required. A thirst that needs quenching.

Perhaps, dear reader, there is a particular photo or story you've heard about some ancestor that tickles the edges of your being? For me, there's a deep, powerful, overriding passion. It's garnet-red like my heart-blood. This pulsing garnet has guided many actions in my life—certainly much of my world travel, and definitely much of my inner inquiry into the question "who am I?"

I had a certain kind of childhood, one that started out free and fun, nature-based, open and loving, but of course, as many childhoods do, churned with many undercurrents of pain, challenge and loneliness.

There was a life-giving spark of a connection, however, that always cracked open the door to my inner self: the twinkle in my grandmother's eye when we were together. My Nana. My Milly. Mildred Gottlieb (Lipton) Zimmerman. We were the apple of each other's eye. After losing her when I was just barely 19, I spent more than the next decade searching for her everywhere else.

I traveled the world to meet my ancestors. I met people in whom I saw myself. I danced for them, I wrote for them, I taught them meditation.

And then, finally, I re-met you, Rifkele, my Nana's cousin.

And here we are in 2020, after a long accumulation of years—over 20 since my Milly died—I am now 40, you are 88, compiling our work to produce this manuscript so that our readers can also find their way into deep, harmonious connection with their ancestors. Or, at the very least, be willing to crack the door on that deep, personal, and intimate resource, that delicious dissonance that may resolve into gorgeous harmony.

For me, writing now on the edge of tears, it is a coming home. *"Devylatchis na vas, ya bachu sebe,"* "In all of you, I see myself." This Ukrainian phrase sings inside of me. In all of you, I see myself, and so, I come home to myself.

I am not you, but I am not *not* you at the same time. I am a tapestry woven of all of our stories, and therefore unique. Because I can come home, my deepest wish is that you too, can return.

Origins. It's so human. So ancient. We've all been longing to come back to ourselves, I mean, haven't we?! Sure, we get caught up by the busyness of life, the intensity of relationships, the turmoil of the climate (political, environmental, societal), and we churn. But where is the deeper meaning? Where is the deeper understanding?

"If not now, when? If not you, who?" If not turn to our ancestors, where can we possibly turn? Hillel the Elder knew to ask this pertinent question, over 2000 years ago.

As an artist myself, a creative, I know that the deepest meaning I experience through creative process are the moments in which I feel connected, tuned in. But what am I dialing into, if not some ancestral, universal human experience?

The music that allows my heart to crack open (even as I write), the paintings that cause me to stop in my tracks, the poems that slay me...what do they all have in common? Heart. Humanity. Depth. A window, a door, a gateway to that which is larger than just my own small mind, my own small experience. Suddenly, in the moment of connection, there is more. There is more, not of *me*, per se, but more that is accessible. There is a *we* that spreads out before me and *that* is richness.

I sit next to you, dear Rifkele, and out of the corner of my eye, you tear a piece of chicken from the bone. This, you might not suspect, brings me to tears. There is no pretense here, no cover up, no shame. We could be back in the shtetl, we could have just killed that chicken to roast for *Shabbos* dinner. There could be the sounds of men studying the *Talmud*.

And this is just my personal experience. But what I suspect is that at our roots, in our essence, we all long for connection. We all long to be seen.

It's about fruition, satisfaction, the ease of loneliness, the balm to the reality that we are alone. If we can at least be seen, witnessed, and *loved,* then there is a *reason* for us to be alive. If one were inclined, one could even say it has to do with *destiny*. And the irony, the hilarious joke of the whole thing is that it's not about the future, but the past. Really, it's about this very moment, this present moment in which we open up and connect. And that's where the joy bubbles from. The sadness is a release into the joy, and that can only happen right here, right now.

So look.

Look.

Look.

Who are you? How did you get here? What makes you thrum with the heat of life and passion and delight? Can you look deeper? Look past those parents that probably burden you with their pain and storylines–look back further, it's in the twinkly sparks of your grandmothers and their grandmother's eyes. Can you see how the lines of their journeys touch you? What of them is in you? What of you is in them? How can this feed you in the deepest sense of all?

I dare you to reach back and feel that life-blood. I dare you to taste the pain and passion, the fear and joy, the fierce loyalty and humanity that runs through your very own blood vessels. In this breath, right here, right now, is the very same air that your ancestors breathed. So breathe deep, my friend, and taste the sunshine.

AND NOW, RIFKE SPEAKS

"The cliche," what is that? Is the phrase overused because it speaks of the *Tale of Two Cities*? The dissonance, the absence of harmony experienced by all the lack of communication contained in a lifetime of seeking agreement, burying the hatchet, the time bomb; pretending to love, to acceptance and to aggressive submission.

So...it may be a cliche, but love is finally all we have in reflecting on the past and where we go with the present. I am amazed that we sit here in 2019 at a table, not a retreat center or a special workshop designed to find that kernel of truth in a silent world...inaction is not the direction to seek anything. Giving up or giving in or silence is not life; it is death. We are here because we want to know who we are and where it all began.

The little child inside does not leave us. The moment we are shoved aside or *act mature* it does not die or disappear, the child is buried but is there. It remains within, always trying to find the escape hatch. The steam that screams in the boiling pot.

We arrived here, you and I, in this country of our birth where other "settlers" already lived, as Jews whose parents spoke another language, who wanted something tangible for themselves, for their children, that "voice" that only our children could develop, could utter, could assimilate into. That cliche is the melting pot. What is that really? Do we melt into a vast reshaping of our lives so the voice that emerges is the sound of marketing sales, a voice of pretending to be an imitation of the accepting sounds of some vast eternal fashion? A style of behavior we need to emulate "dress for success" or, use that "winning smile."

We found ourselves wanting to rescue the voice or voices of the *real* place we came from...the piece of land that was our ancestor's spot...the goat, or donkey they had in the small village they were born in and from which they fled. The piano, the museum, the theatre was the cultural horizon our families sought here. The essence that remains may be buried inside a simple, silent, human being who contains that collective voice, that unconscious spirit of what was and what is.

So…we found each other, so different and yet so joined. My childhood, the first generation Jewish girl and your grandmother, the first in her small family circle. My mother loved your great grandmother. They spoke every day; I listened, I heard, I was a *"gutah madelle,"* and your grandmother was that older cousin sailing, I believed, through a gilded cave, or was it a cage…She had a cute boyfriend, a joyous life (or so I thought). They babysat me and my recollection of my admiration for these special older kids is a continuing voice in my life.

I was a self-developed imposter at 8 or 9 years old. Who brought me to Sarah? The same cousin to visit me years later with this golden child…her special little girl in a lifetime of boys, sons and grandsons. I wanted to know this child especially after her grandmother died suddenly, but not unexpectedly. Could we, the young woman and an old woman find our truth together in the sea of pretense, and denial? If we could do it, anyone could…again, if *they could love themselves, and love each other.*

The tale of the Jews in America is, for me, a foreign voice in a sea of pretense. We are better than them, we are brighter than them, we know more than they do. But do we really feel that being Jewish is OK? If so, why do we deny our backgrounds and try to emulate some model we don't understand?

I decided to study English literature—after all, the English speak the language better than we do, they are more polite, superior people…their theatre is better than ours so we must imitate it, change our names, change our noses, change into something superior…that Cambridge Don, that better brand…The Jewish cantorial voice, the search to escape to the special college or university founded by Christians from the "High Church."

Here is my cousin's grandchild, not afraid of knowing the deeper truth. The *shtetl* is deeply embedded in our hearts.

It is a voice of memory for my buried love for my father, the relative that links Sarah and I together. He was the singer, the tortured revolutionary who worked himself into early death. But as he raged against "the system," he loved poetry, music, tipping the rowboat. He could love fun, he could be an emissary of joy.

Yes, I *could* love Sarah for herself, for her joy in the search, for her tremendous capacity to be honest and to be loving and to *really mean what she says*...WOW!

Perhaps a more important part of our Jewish heritage is that we always had to "be right." We *never* admitted failure as friends or parents or in our work life. It was always "the other." We needed to justify our own actions, our state of justification.

Now we meet as generations apart yet able to confront ourselves and remember those we hurt and those we have loved. Again, oh well. "Love" is the anchor to our life's experience.

Sarah has left the children and travelled over 5 hours to be with me...writing together because if we don't do it, who will?

Her grandmother, my admired cousin, struggled through her own pain. That great couple I viewed as a child did not last through a long and happy marriage. It fell apart by anxiety and then betrayal and "no-one should ever know." Our mothers *never* spoke again. How could her mother tell mine that her daughter was divorced? The rest was silence...

But, yes, love can "conquer all" and Sarah's grandmother and I became close again and Sarah is this incredible voice for love, for strong bonds, for embracing our past and our own voices of our imperfections.

Can anyone change? I'm called naive because I believe we can. The emotional poverty in those European ghettos was not joyous and comradely embracing of life, particularly for women. It was narrow and confining and constrictive. We are all afraid of the inner voice. But *we* have, we hope, found a truth, and one we can share.

So what can we discover and what can we rescue of the creativity and love that we shared, eventually? Does the honesty, the truth of our "American" experience negate or explain the special categorical system of the qualities of this time, and my Yiddish sense of self?

It was that special "caste" system that protected millions of Jews who left Russia-Poland before the Holocaust because no self-protective fraud (denial) could convince them they were invincible or could survive the atrocities of their humiliating life experiences.

We are here at this table, Sarah and I, because we continued to want to engage in the struggle to find that elusive identity by choice. The golden child, now adult woman is herself a strong survivor.

Denial? Interwoven with our
    daily movements
Can we deal with the death
    that awaits us?
Can we Know we breathe
    temporary air
Before the inevitable erasure
Oblivion when our lives
    cease
Sarah dreams of her menorah
    and tuba
I dream of total nullification
Nothing left
My pretense for inactivity and sloth

CHAPTER ONE: LET'S BE HONEST

Writing is a process. Let's be honest. How we dive into the stream of story will determine how we experience the river of our life.

As you will see, dear reader, Rifke and I meander back and forth in the following pages. Gaining familiarity with each other and with the process of slowly picking apart our inheritance, we slowly reveal an honesty and depth heretofore untasted.

The journey is raw. It's deeply personal. But we hope there's enough inspiration in here for you to keep reading, and by swimming with us, you too turn to listen to the whispering voices of your own ancestors, and thereby also receive the gift of truly learning who you are. We now begin our journey into the power of connection here in the middle of a stream, ancestors connecting into the present moment, building bridges to the future, bridges we hope, that are of benefit. What follows is an unfolding correspondence of reconnection between our generations.

We recognize this is not a thoroughly polished work. We know that it meanders. We worked to bring themes together, and sometimes we shifted the placement of a piece of writing in the stream of time because that piece was needed to tie a thread of the story together. Bear with us. Life is messy, and it's in the journey itself that we find meaning.

OCTOBER 23, 2015 – RIFKE

I feel we should be as honest about our pasts, our inheritance, our beliefs, our prejudices as we can. Yes...we are finally sitting after so many years in our house in Norwalk, CT. The question beyond all other ageless questions is, "Why write this book?"

After thinking about all the inevitable issues of love and death, I do believe that you are destined to carry on the painful and often joyous tradition of a fiddler—or, if you prefer—trombonist on a roof.

We are sitting side by side with your baby asleep against your warm and loving breast and we are thinking about meaning. We have no real central ideology: we both fervently feel we should seek a truth about going on, about cherishing human warmth, about keeping alive inner values and not dictating our own particular sense of correctness as knowledge. We both know that there is no central way to living a life because as individuals we come to our knowledge base from totally different places.

I don't even know why I have always tried to connect with you but I do know I have loved you. Even when we did not speak or communicate, I held on to my memory of you. My close childhood cousin, my admired older musical cousin, Mildred (12 years older than me) had this delicate, lovely quiet little grandchild named Sarah. I was not close with the middle generation, your parents, but I always held close in my gut to Mildred and to you.

We attended your wedding ceremony in Maine and yet I am so completely a secular Jew so far to the left politically. Yet we both separately did work in areas of Asia that are not chic or popular or frequented by Americans. You are married to a kind and lovely man, not a Jew, and I am married to Bill, a Jew by choice. His mother was a Jew born in Lithuania but wanting to escape that *shtetl*, rebelled and married a non-Jewish Russian.

When I held your daughter Odessa I wanted to sing to her in Yiddish. I wanted to give you my chicken. I wanted to be your close cousin because I also loved your Nana, Mildred, when I was a child. I am overwhelmed with the truth that our persistence, mostly my insistence, that we get together has met at this final juncture and we need to share the roots. Please know I will continue...

OCTOBER 30, 2015 – SARAH

I pause and turn again towards that doorway to the past. It is always over my shoulder, my left one I believe. I always knew you and I were connected, Rifke, and I am so thankful that we have had the opportunity to reconnect out of space and time and meet in this place of words and memories.

I was the apple of my Nana's eye, did you know that? She was my savior in my turbulent teenage years. She was overwhelming to me when I was a child because I was a staunch tom-boy and she wanted me to like diamonds and roses and all things girly. I didn't like that, and I didn't like that she made me pose for pictures all the time, and in fact, I'm still a little ruined by photos and don't want to do the same thing to my daughter. But I grew out of the tom-boy-only phase and grew into myself as a woman, choosing to create a wedding band out of Nana's gold and jewels. The crown jewel of my wedding ring is one of her own diamonds. So she is always with me, always present in my heart and on my hand.

It did not help that my mother had a very difficult time with Nana. It did not help that my father was…I am not even sure what, but they had an enmeshed kind of relationship. What helped was when Nana moved to be close to us in her last years, and then she and I were able to develop our own intimate connection. I had never had a close grandparent until then, and I relished every second of it. She was funny, really hilarious. She'd make the silliest jokes and we'd laugh and laugh and laugh. But she also had an ear for my more serious concerns, and when I was stretching the boundaries, she'd accept me for exactly who I was. Every time.

I always knew she loved you, Rifke. She would laugh and talk about times from when you were both young, and she'd even tell me stories about boyfriends she had before she met my Grandpa.

And somehow, I am so drawn to her mother, Merele. I think maybe it is because of the inheritance of the Menorah. When I traveled to Israel to meet our distant cousins there, I was shocked to learn that Yehudit, Merele's mother, who gave her the menorah (and which I like to believe she had saved from her mother's mother's mother), had died a week after arriving in Palestine to visit her other two daughters. There I was in the desert, visiting my great-great grandmother's grave. This woman whose blood I share, whose name I cherish, and who I can only meet through dreams.

I believe it is through Yehudit's parents that we are related, is that correct?

I feel sometimes that the Vilna Gaon, our very distant ancestor, is also resting just on the edge of my vision, often prompting me to think even more deeply, to mull over meaning and not to just speculate, but to know. I feel this presence as encouragement, and it intermingles with my life's practice as a Buddhist. I do not feel that being a Buddhist is in anyway an insult to my Jewish heritage, but is rather informed by it. We Jews are used to deep inquiry, are we not?

It is the writing time, when autumn leaves have fallen and the land is again bare and barren. I love to see the shape of the hills, their bones laid bare and ready for plucking. It is the writing time, and I cannot tell you how deeply thrilled I am to be writing with you, my cousin, my long-lost and distant relation. I have been waiting for many, many years to write this with you, and even as I am here on this Vermont hilltop, I feel you sitting by my side.

ENTER: THE VOICE OF OUR STORY

We flip forward in time for a moment to bring clarity around the ancestral story that brought us into connection in the present. We move forward in time to move backwards in time...

FEBRUARY 10, 2019 – SARAH

The story my Nana always told me was that her parents walked out of Russia. I do not know, and can not corroborate if that was true. I do know that they likely walked down Potemkin's Steps in Odessa, Ukraine to get to the ship that would take them sailing away from Russia. I do know that when I stood there, exactly 100 years after they had walked those stairs, that I could feel the streaming thousands that had walked those stairs before me. I could feel the fear, anxiety and freedom, the release, the sense of unshackling from the past and stepping into the unknown future.

The two threads of my father's lineage—the intelligentsia from Pinsk and the merchants from Ekaterinaslav (current day Dnipropetrovsk)—were both focused on love, loyalty, survival and craft. The Pinsk family is the one I have always focused on in my heart, likely I am sure because of my connection with Milly and through her, to Merele and Yehudit. The Lipshitz from Ekaterinaslav, merchants with the smarts to know they needed to upend the entire clan and ship out to America, were passionate.

The stories of the Lipshitz, and the repeating patterns that have cycled through all five generations that I know about, all seem to go back to the origins of the city of Ekaterinaslav. Perched high on a hill above a gorgeous bend in the river Dnieper, the city was claimed and named by Potemkin in the 1700s for his illicit lover, Catherine the Great, Empress of Russia. The city was founded on illicit love. When I stood there in the palace Potemkin built for Katarina, 100 years after my family fled the "storms" of the pogroms, I could feel the sweeping tide of time and love and pain. Five generations ago, my great-great grandfather told his wife, "I'm just going out for a pack of smokes," probably in Yiddish, and he didn't come back for two years. That was after they had all emigrated to New York, changed their name, as a family of 30 to Lipton, and ran a market called "Lipton's Market". You couldn't have opened a grocery in New York City called "Liptshitz" in the 1920s.

His son, my great-grandfather Sam (who married his first cousin Goldie) was a well-known womanizer (as the story goes), and there is some speculation in the family that he may have actually wooed and slept with his son's mother-in-law, my very own Merele. Aaron, my grandfather, Sam's eldest son, fell in love early with Mildred—they were high school sweethearts—and kept that flame alive when he was in the WWII in the South Pacific as a radio operator. I have photos he sent of him looking very sultry and attractive with cute little phrases on the back of the photos he sent to her. Then, when my father was 13, Aaron fell in love with his high school secretary (he was the Principal), and left my Nana, which devastated the family. Rhona was nearly 20 years younger than he. They went on to have three more children (which for me is wonderful because that's why I have wonderful young aunties!!).

My father then turned around and left my family when I was 16, shacking up with a woman exactly the same age difference of his father and Rhona. His brother did the same thing.

My brother, my cousin and I have all had our own relationships with this pattern.

And the thread that remains constant is love, and passion.

Who we are is not a given.

But, of course, we are so thoroughly infused with who we were, which is to say, who our ancestors were. I truly believe that you and I see what we need in one another because we want to. Because, who else can see it? So in this, we are extremely fortunate because we have discovered the secret magic of creating the world as we want it to be. This is a magic that is beyond time, beyond life and death. Just as Mildred is always hovering at my shoulder and reminding me to laugh, we shall persevere together.

CHAPTER TWO: THE IRRITATION OF DISSONANCE

If we do not lean into the exposure of irritation, we do not become clear to ourselves. Longing to open, we have to lean in, and listen.

NOVEMBER 2, 2015 – SARAH

Irritation arises. Is it the lack of leaves which causes the more blustery wind to whip through my once-protected meadow? Is it the longing for independence, which I knew for so long before having this beautiful and occasionally aggravating baby? Is it wishing that I could hear my Nana's voice? Is it the dissonance of Bartok? The chill of November?

The longing to know all the stories but being faced with having to craft many of them on my own gives way to the sometimes-trust that the stories I make up are actually plucked from the ether, and therefore told to me by my ancestors. It is my job to listen. Listening is what I have trained for. It is what I offer in my work, it is the best offering I can give to my baby, my husband, my family, and it is how I have learned to find the stories. Patience is the requirement, and not always easy to come by.

I do feel it is my burden and delight to both know myself and also know that I MUST BE myself. It has always been this way for me, and I have also always felt that it was an expression of my female ancestors. But I never knew or understood until just this moment in reading your words, Rifke, why that was so loaded.

I feel so strongly about being who I am that I never really stopped to think that my ancestors did not, could not.

Pretend it exists?! Who does that! Know it and be it, that's what I've always said. But perhaps the pain that I have inherited is that stain of pretending, and anytime that I begin to feel that cloud drift over the sun, the reason I baulk so loudly is because I KNOW it is not the whole story.

Be who you are. That is the premise of the work I am building. Empowering others to be and lead from who they are. (Note, we began writing this book four years before birthing GENUINE, my online community intently focused on teaching people how to #bewhoyouare.)

Connecting deeply to our own roots, both in this present moment—embodying our experience—and also on the earth—paying homage to our ancestors—this is what allows us to lead and go forward. But perhaps this is a luxury and my ancestors had to look forward only to their next day's bread, the hearth that needed tending, the candle that needed dripping, the daughter that needed encouraging, the son that needed reminding.

Perhaps, in this 21st Century, I have the supreme luxury to not only be who I am but also be a guide for others to be who they are. Do you think my ancestors would champion this? Do you think they would be proud? Satisfied? Gratified that their labors came to this particular fruition. Deep in my heart, I think probably *yes*.

And I must trust this. I must tap-dance this tune as loudly and ferociously as possible. I know that I have reaped the benefit of other's suffering before me. That Nana once had a dream, I know. She told me about it. It revolved around the cello. And then she had a terrible, abusive teacher, and she fell off the rail and into domesticity. But she found her voice again, later, in the teacher's union in New York. She had passion, she had bluster, she had courage, though maybe it bloomed late.

Merele too had a dream, a vision, a passion. She found a ticket out of Russia and did not sell her whole soul. She too longed for music, and brought Mildred to all the music she could find. Being a milliner was just to pay the bills. Being married to Morris was just the ticket away from the Pogroms. She found her satisfaction, I like to believe, in Mildred's making of music. Mildred then found her satisfaction in her son's music. And Jonathan still carries that burden, and that flame. I do too, to a different degree. For me, the music is more metaphorical. I follow it, but it guides me down twisting and unconventional roads.

I wonder, would Merele recognize me as her own?

This is potent, powerful, real and deep. I have been longing for this kind of dialogue for all of my life. Interesting that it had to wait until now, me just nine months into being a Mama.

DECEMBER 4, 2015 – SARAH, RIFKE

SARAH

There was snow on the ground when I woke up this morning! It was so beautiful. And as I was looking out the window, I saw two deer walk across the lawn, heading straight for the apple trees. I was happy we hadn't picked all of them earlier in the autumn, glad that they would have a delicious winter meal on this snowy morning.

How are you? I haven't heard from you in a while and wanted to make sure everything is good. I long for more writing from you and with you!

Would you be willing to write a little bit about what you remember of my great-grandmother? I feel so drawn to Merele, so drawn to this woman who in my mind started out soft and ended up stoic. I don't know much about her and can't really ask my dad right now. I feel like I have a good grasp of my Nana, of who she was and what made her tick. Re-reading her "memoirs" (which I typed up so I could send to you - did you see that?), brought her close to my mind again. But Merele, I don't know about her too much. I know that she visited her sisters in Palestine and got stuck there for the 7 day war in the 40s, so I know she remained close in some way with her disparate family. But what made her tick? What was she like as a woman? As a mother?

What do you know?

And what is the import for *you* in writing about this funny family we share?

RIFKE

I have been thinking about our heritage and our fierce love since I read your words. Can one "love" too deeply or too much? Do we drive away our sons (children) because we love them so totally and without any control or restraint? Is this really the case? I used to think so. Now I believe that letting go is the real love. Control is a perversion of love.

Mildred was a Jewish, urban woman. She did not enjoy Maine or sailing or camping or the great outdoors. She could not stand the sun and feared the winters. She went to be near David. You know the rest of that painful story. Love must also be tender and reciprocal and respectful and just generally appreciated. What is that Jewish love of the sons? Is it that the son is the Kaddish and recites the prayer for the dead. Is it the transfer of love for husband to son? Is it the hope the son will heal?

We "found"each other again because we both wanted to. Bill and I came to your wedding because we just knew we could not "miss" it. You were never another sweet or glib young woman. You have been the seeker. I knew it would never be just another relative showing up and another smile and thank you note.

Mildred and I really followed very different roads or paths. I always wanted a cousin, a deep friendship, a sister spirit. She gained depth because she loved you and you are fearless. How did that happen? How did you grow into the complex person you are? Certainly not from your parents or grandparents. I think from your own courage. I am so proud of you and feel so wonderful about our openness and good faith and authenticity,

This poem, I believe, illustrates the feelings (at least my own) growing up in the pain and loss our Jewish parents felt during the holocaust... They spoke to each other about the situation but never to the "kinder." At all costs they must be spared and have culture, not awareness. The best Baldwin or Steinway piano and always books by Steinbeck or Dreiser or Shakespeare or... another great writer.

Linen Jacket

    The white, linen jacket
    A hand me down
    Lovely, crisp, free moving
    Large
    I grabbed it whenever I was invited
    For a drive to anywhere
    I was six or maybe five
    Loving to go away -
    Away from the sadness,
    Pain, holocaust remembrance
    Dead - all gone - never to return
    From the fire, frenzy, searching through
    Chaos and death in Europe
    Somewhere .
    I recall
    Rumble seat car
    I was considered cute, acceptable, cheerful
    Invited
    I'd go anywhere
    Anyway.

So you see Sarah I cannot revise the history I lived through and I still did love Mildred and wanted desperately to have her in *my* life. She was the cousin I admired and she was admitted to the New York High School of Music and Art. That was my goal... to play the cello even though I was recommended to the flute. All "water under some bridge."

Mary was close to my mother but she was not revealing any of her inner self. She seemed to have contempt for Morris who hung around my father's drug store and felt he was alienated to the "two women." I saw him as a well dressed man who was intensely lonely and shut out of Mildred's and Mary's life. Mary lived for Mildred, when I was old enough to observe. She did not go on with any life of her own, I thought. She was good looking and tall (from my vantage point), and always needing comfort from my mother.

DECEMBER 2, 2015 – SARAH

An anniversary has come and gone - 11 years since my mom died. I asked my brother lots of questions about mom. I almost never do that. She was annoying and controlling and irritating, but she was also my mother and therefore there was a lot of sweetness. She was very creative, and I think I've inherited that in large measure from her. Creative in the sense of pushing the bounds and limits, finding new ways to do things.

I recently have found myself being asked to do lots of different things (even if they are just conversations with people) and I have had to say no. In fact, I just spent the morning saying no to six different people for six different things. I was all torn in knots beforehand, not wanting to hurt feelings or disappoint. I want so much to be all-accommodating, but the truth is, I cannot be, and should not be. I must be available to my daughter and my husband and my close circle of family and friends (of which I number you), but I also must be available for my business. And it has to be up to me what to accept and reject. And it's rare that I reject. I hate being rejected as well, and so feel even worse about it. What is this burden that I feel I must be all-accommodating? Is this something I have inherited from these Jewish women?

The poem you sent about the linen jacket touched me deeply. The memories and the pain of the Holocaust are something I have been savagely drawn to all of my life. I think it is for the very fact that nobody in my family would talk about it. Nana wouldn't say much, just waving her hand saying something like, oh we don't talk about that. I know that her mother wouldn't talk about it, that she wouldn't talk about the old country, except maybe to mumble something in Yiddish. This, I only imagine. I look to you to fill in some details - who was Merele? Who was she in this new country? Who was she as a housewife who didn't like her husband? Who was she after Morris left (and why and how did he go?)? I know from Nana her passion for music, but the rest I know is only imagined.

Ever since I was a small child, I would read as many books as I could about stories of survivors from the Holocaust. In some part of me, there is the belief that I was alive at that time and escaped to Sweden; I felt that when I visited Denmark and had an uncanny experience crossing the sound to Sweden. I also feel that I have the burden/joy/task of remembering, of "carrying" the memories so that they will not die. I am the one in my immediate family who always cared about the stories, and am the one that is burdened with keeping all of the photo albums (oh, how I would love to ship them off to someone to scan so we can print them into books and I can get rid of the physical burden of so many decaying boxes).

Irritation with people who are a little slow, this too I think is something I get from Nana. I see so far, so big, so quickly, that I get very irritated when someone is stuck in small mind. This is not a good trait for someone like me who is a teacher! I have to have more patience—for myself and for others!

Perhaps the irritation is with the rain on this cloudy, cold December day. At least my baby girl makes me smile through my whole body!

DECEMBER 3, 2015 – RIFKE

I am more actively involved in the ritual of Judaism because of the holocaust and because I always feel (and felt) the onslaught of anti-semitism from the Puritan tradition and the theme of the scarlet letter and the burning of witches. I guess it is powerfully developed by Shirley Jackson in *The Lottery* and Arthur Miller in *The Crucible*.

Why dirty Jew? Why the superiority of the formidable Protestants? How many of us (me included) believed we were inferior? Blond, tall, slim, self-contained, stoic, the symbol was Bowdoin College or Wellseley or...? Then we discover, Mildred and I, that we are O.K. even though we do not have these attributes.

More significantly, are they attributes? It is wonderful to love and to cry and to laugh and to be a divergent thinker... a Chagall, a *Sholem Aleichem*?

CHAPTER THREE: SURVIVING AMONGST SHARDS

Too much pain has been covered up in our lives. When we actually let ourselves see it, acknowledge it and feel it, we free ourselves from the chains that bind.

The metaphors that resonate for us may begin to haunt us, but when we lean into them, we are revealed to ourselves.

NOVEMBER 2, 2015 – SARAH

Stamina and survival. Yes, I can feel these two things, and feel how interestingly they compete, work in tandem with, and also conflict with my own mother's Puritan heritage. Survival was so much a part of the journey, but celebration was also needed. How do you celebrate when you are so focused on survival? I've always felt that Hannukah was about celebration, that the candles in the menorah were a celebration of light, of life, of love and connection. But I did not study Jewish catechism, so I do not remember the traditional tales. My placement of my inherited menorah has always been the most honored, the most sacred place in my home. Was this silver object one of celebration, survival or pure remembrance?

DECEMBER 3, 2015 – RIFKE, SARAH

> *Regina*
> We compose
> Our lives
> From the shards of troubled paths
> Lies, subterfuge, escape
> "Let's Pretend" games
> Of childhood
> Of mangled dreams
> Fears, destruction

Cloaked in pristine
Behavior, smiling at the cameras
Once in a long array of performances
Fathers - mothers - history
Some of us discover
A moment of hope!

Sarah
We compose
our lives
from the shreds of
someday's promise
basking in brilliance
and clarity of mind.

We compose
our lives
like spiders
at the center
the web
rotating
around us
in spirals.

Cloaked in threads
of 10,000 colors
we radiate
possibility
forgiveness
and trust.

The dance
of our ancestors -
the rhythm
the beat
the pulse
the blood

Coursing
through
our
veins.

DECEMBER 5, 2015 – RIFKE

I can't believe it! I missed your response and believed you were "blowing it off." Not me but our subject matter. Your response is so how I feel about trying to "please" everyone because we ourselves are so sensitive to rejection. That is the key! Yes, I think our background in the holocaust affected Mildred and then the way she raised your father, David. I can't believe you have found inner clarity at such a young, developing age. I only experienced your mother as wanting to be "superior" and very cruel. She made fun of Mildred behind her back. She must have also suffered from low self-esteem. We can do it together.

DECEMBER 7, 2015 – SARAH

And so it is, we write to find the answer to our ancient question. That is it!

I have long wondered why it is I feel so compelled to write, to search, to dream my ancestors. This has been both burden and delight in my life. And it has finally arrived that it is pure delight. Writing with you, dear Rifke, is the proof in the pudding!

Sure, there may be acid in my stomach about my parents. Sure, there are shards of glass when I think of the strained relationship between my mother and my Nana. Sure, there are many moments of betrayal and rage.

But, and here's where the delight comes in, I am ALIVE! And beyond that, I have had the profound joy and opportunity to bring to life another small, gorgeous being. The fact that we are alive and can love and dance and laugh and cry and experience the cold of winter and the warmth of sun, the chimes singing a beautiful lullaby to the baby on my back, these are the facts of life. That we can eat hot soup and warm up, that we can let go of the question and let the answers come tumbling in. This is the poem, the story, the song.

This is what I want my children to inherit: this love of the questioning itself, this passion for knowing that we are a lineage that streams far, far back into the distance of time.

The Longing
I know
bent back
leaning forward
the weight of
ancestors
and to-do lists
the burden of
caring.

I also know
upright back
support of ancestors
encircling
the warmth
of sleeping baby
the weightlessness
of water
the delight
of connection.

DECEMBER 10, 2015 – RIFKE

Just a brief comment in the middle of our discourse. I love you, dear Sarah.

Shards of Glass…Moments of Anger
I grasp, weakly, uncertain
The body I still possess.
I walk, chat, question
Dangerously circling the air
   Not as ballerina
But blind and ancient
Sounds in my head
"Yes, I am someone!"

Who?
Not a Moslem woman
Sheathed in shawls, scarves and
Modesty.
Not a fashion icon
Teasing the photoshoot

With cleavage and jewels
Just a breathing, searching
Bent woman
With a dim lamp
Devoted to finding
That answer to our ancient question.

ENTER: THE VOICE OF MILDRED ZIMMERMAN

I begged my Nana to share stories with me. Women of her generation and earlier were very tight-lipped about the past. Too much pain to share, they felt. "It's all in the past, what does it matter," she would say.

But she knew that I longed to know and so she tried for me. Here is a sample of what she wrote by hand for me, two years before she died.

MEMOIRS FOR SARAH, A VERY LONG LETTER

BEGUN APRIL 10, 1997
[transcribed from the original handwritten diary]

My wonderful granddaughter:
You have been urging me to "tell you my stories" for a long time—I always wanted to—and told you little bits and pieces as they came to mind. But I do understand your need to know and—before my memory possibly erodes—I better get started.

The temptation, when you're writing a memoir, is to tell only the stories that make you feel the hero—or make you shine—but that's not always the whole story, so I'll try very hard to be honest and tell it all—the good, the bad and the ugly too, if necessary. I hope you won't think less of me when the "uglies" appear, but everyone I know has some in their life, so no point in not telling all.

I suppose the beginning should be with what I know of my parents—lots of gaps in that story. Anyway Mary (probably Miriam at birth—changed to Mary by Ellis Island officials) was born in Pinsk, Russia in 1892. She was the middle daughter with an older and a younger sister (Hanze and Rivke or Rivele) and three brothers (I don't know their ages or even their names). Their parents—(Abraham and Judit (Judith) Karzinell) had a dry goods store where they sold bolts of material: buttons, and so on. They lived in Pinsk, which was a town that apparently bred an intellectual and maybe a bit revolutionary group of young Jews. My aunts, Hanze and Rivele, fell in love with

Zionists and in about 1909 or 1910 went to what was then Palestine to farm the land, and so on.

The brothers never left Pinsk, probably became somewhat involved with the early Russian revolutionists of the time. They stayed, married, and seemingly lived well until World War II and the Nazis came and killed them all.

My mother at 17 fell in love with a woodchopper's son, Morris Gottlieb, who emigrated to America with his parents, Pincus and Ida in about 1908-1910. Russia, at that time (or ever) was not too friendly to Jews—remember "Fiddler on the Roof"? The Cossacks would come through every once in a while and burn a village, rape a few girls, then ride off. My mother remembered one such Pogrom (as it was called) and escaped the Cossacks by running to the river and hiding there.

Anyway, Morris wanted her to come to America and even though her family was not too crazy about Morris (he was, after all, not an intellectual), she packed and in 1910 came to America. Morris had some cousins in Cleveland, Ohio and they were married there in 1910. Morris had a sister Fanny who married a pharmacist (family name Silver) and they lived in Fargo, North Dakota. We used to write to each other and, in all the years, we only met once: in the late 70's. I thought we had a pleasant meeting, but somehow I guess she didn't think so because despite the many letters I wrote afterward she never answered. My feeling is that she, being married to a big-shot doctor in Minneapolis was not overly impressed with her union-made cousin. Sad, but what's to do?

Back to the story. Mary and Morris moved to New York, he to work as a pattern-maker in the garment district, and she to be a homemaker. Somewhere, around 1915-16 a daughter named Esther was born. Sadly she had a "soft" head. The skull bones (fontanel) never joined. She never even sat up and she would have been mentally retarded. Maybe, for that era, it was merciful that she died at 16 months.

A son, Albert, was born in 1918 (or '19) and thrived until 5 years old. I was born in 1923 and when I was one year old, Albert came down with leukemia, one week after he entered kindergarten. I can only begin to imagine the shock and pain his death was to my parents. My mother said in my later years that she turned gray overnight and my father never spoke to me about it. I grew up as my mother's darling and with very little relationship with my father. He horsed around with me, but rarely. I have some sharp memories of him. Once, I came upon him drunk at the table and crying over and over, "Oh, my son, my son." I was too young (maybe 6 or 7) to understand him and when my mother shooed me away, I was left with the feeling that he was angry at me for being a girl and living, when his son was gone. Yet, I never was angry or jealous of Albert. I remember fantasizing that he was my guardian angel and was watching over me always. No one ever spoke to me about Albert, so he was always just in my head.

I always wished I had hair that would grow to my waist. It never (even as an adult) grew past my neck, so when I was supposed to be asleep I would drape one of my mother's long chiffon scarves over my head, arrange all my dolls (I had a lot) around my bed, parade around the room, pretending my brother Albert, was sitting there too, and talk to him and the dolls.

A GLASS OF TEA

When I was real little (3 or 4) my "Zeydah" (Grandfather), my father's father came to live with us. My grandmother Ida was in a nursing home (I don't know why). He had red hair and a long red/gray beard. My mother, out of respect for his beliefs, kept a kosher house.

He adored me. He called me "Molleleh." He spoke Yiddish and Russian, so the little Yiddish I recall was from him. If my mother went out, he would take care of me and, as soon as she was out the door, he'd say, "A glussale tea, Molleleh" (translation: a glass of tea). The Russians drank tea in a glass with a lump of hard sugar in their teeth to run the tea through. For me he'd put dark cherry preserves in the glass (yummy!).

Many, many years later at a Russian restaurant (still there) right near Carnegie Hall in New York—called "the Russian Tea Room"—waiters dressed in Russian blouses served tea in a glass with cherries. I had some there and nearly cried into the tea.

Then we'd go out for a walk and often (back inside) he'd play with me and let me climb up his beard. He was with us a year or two and then (I think my dear old Dad threw him out); he moved to live with some distant relatives in Richmond, Virginia, where he worked as a Shamas (like a general caretaker or assistant) in a small orthodox "shul" (synogogue).

We visited once and I recall walking down the street and wondering at the barefoot little black kids running around. He also bought me a tiny little scissors. When I was 7, we heard that he had died and I remember being very upset because my father wouldn't even go to his funeral. To this day I remember my Zaydeh warmly—with love.

THE PIANO

During the depression in (in the 30's) we moved from a nice building (1 Sickles Street) which had an elevator - down the street to 20 Sickles Street—an older building, with smaller room and a walk-up, three floors.

My father had a hard time keeping a job and I do remember once seeing a long line of men and my mother telling me that was a "soup line."

Despite all that, I don't remember ever being without food—or piano lessons. My mother bought a piano (remember the one in Hartsdale?) and paid it out over the years. My piano teacher, a heavy man with stubby fingers, charged very little. He also owned a children's camp (Camp High Point) in the Catskill Mountains, New York, and when I was 9 or 10, I went there for a few summers. I loved it. We had a lake and boats. I played softball and swam. I loved it.

I did well in school. I'd get an "A" in work and sometimes a "C" in conduct (because I talked too much). The meanest thing a teacher ever did to me was when I was in 1st or 2nd grade. In those days our desks and seats were screwed down to the floor and the boys sat in rows separated from the girls' rows. Also the "smart" kids sat in the first row. Well, I was smart! I had first row, first seat (wow-ee!). Then one day, I really had to go to the bathroom (I was barely graduated from a long-time bed-wetting problem) and I was waving my hand furiously. "You will wait a while" said my dear teacher. But, I persisted in waving my hand - till she finally said "If you can't wait, then go, but you will lose your seat for it." So I went. I really did have to go and, sure enough, when I *returned, every kid had moved back a seat and I had the first row, second seat. No one ever had the first seat again. Boy, what a sadist she was!*

So I went through elementary school and then Junior High. I always had other girls to play with. One girl, Barbara Lifflander, and I did quite naughty things. Once, we were in her apartment, filling small paper bags with water and dropping them down on people walking by. We'd throw and duck! We never even got caught! (This episode was some years before Junior High.)

Sadly, that was as much as my Nana was willing or able to write...

And that is why I have had to lean in and listen to the whispers of my ancestors...

CHAPTER FOUR: LISTENING TO OUR ANCESTORS

When we lean in to listen to the voices whispering to us, no matter how shadowy, we learn. The more we learn, the more we grow. The dance reveals the joy. The stories reveal the pain. The tapestry reveals the meaning of life...

DECEMBER 11, 2015 – SARAH

Happy Hanukkah! We lit the menorah last night, not the ancestral one, but the simple one I grew up with. Odessa clapped with delight at seeing the flames! We turned out all the lights and sang Hanukkah songs, and we stayed to watch the candles burn all the way down. It felt so wonderful to share this beautiful holiday of light with her, it was always my favorite one!!

Every day, because of our writing, I feel I am listening to ancestors. I can feel the women of our lineage, but not really the men. This is interesting only because I realize that I am so focused on the women of our lineage, and I almost don't care about the men. Do you feel this way? Do you know what I mean?

I feel we are asking the right questions, getting at the root of who we are as Russian Jewish Women. Capital Women, with large hearts, nice round bellies, and stories galore. Please, keep writing!!

The sun is shining and it is bizarrely warm for December. I have walked many miles this week with Odessa strapped to my back.

FEBRUARY 8, 2019 – SARAH

The years have spiraled and we have delved deeply into our own journey of connection. Now, let us turn the pages of time back and investigate the story of our ancestors, those who have conspired to bring us back.

But telling a family story, this is a complicated thing. It's not just the facts, though you've seen what my Milly was able to share. It's the patterns, the atmosphere, the pain that tell the story. And it's also the sparks that shine through that pain, the humor that rises out of the ashes.

Rifke sits next to me asking me: "How did you become a person out of all of those lies and pain?" I laugh, look out the window at sun glancing off icy water and say, "it's because we lean into the questions!" It's because I lean into the questions that I even *have* a semblance of a story to tell.

Sure, I have to craft my own glimmering sense of our ancestor's story, because nobody actually spoke about the pain. I have to recreate my sense of their location because I have been there. I don't actually know what the dust tasted like. I don't actually know the horror of a pogrom witnessed. I don't actually know why there was so much sadness. But I also *do know*. I know that my great-grandmother lost two children after she arrived in this new country. I know that she never saw her parents again. I know that she traveled just once to Israel to see her sisters and meet their families. I know that there was devastation when she lost her father and brothers and their families to the Holocaust. I know why she never talked about any of it - she couldn't. It's too much. Too much loss. Too much of the same loss everyone around her was also experiencing.

And so the culture that we create out of that - the piano lessons, the Steinway piano bought, the Leonard Bernstein concerts attended, the cello purchased, the museums visited, the Yiddish spoken, the candles bought and burned, not as rich as the mother's home-made candles...the deeper questions a luxury not to indulge in.

And so time spirals forward and though patterns repeat, questions start to stir and arise and I become a child who asks. A child who wants to *know*. A child who devours every story about World War II that I can get my hands on. I become a student of music and art and poetry, always wanting to travel, always wanting to know what *your* experience is. Because, as I have learned, in all of you, I see myself.

And so I dance the journey, not because I am the end of the story, no, but because through me you can live and grow and dance, unshackled from patterns, but aware of their existence, aware of all the richness and resource and delight that is right at your fingertips if only you let it in.

Ever the tuba player supporting the rest of the orchestra with rich harmony and occasional dissonance, I perform so that you can dance in freedom.

OCTOBER 26, 2015 – SARAH

There is a door over my shoulder. I look to the left, letting my gaze stray through it. There is a feeling of being summoned and I turn slowly, letting go of what is in front of me. I decide to spend some time in this shimmering place. I put down the pencil and paper, and turn towards that beckoning door. In the distance I see a river glimmering in the sunshine, dappled by the eastern trees along its banks. Next to the river is a small shtetl I know, it's Pinsk. Living there is a large family, an old family, my family.

Off to the right I hear a voice calling, "Merele! Merele!" It is mother Yehudit. The baking is done, and it is time to set the Shabbos candles on the table. This is before, before the end was coming.

In a field nearby there are some woodmen working, harvesting the logs from that day's felling. In the distance, among the breezes are the family's gardens. Lavender and jasmine wafting their beautiful scents in the air. These last are for the soaps that mama Yehudit is going to make. Abraham and Isaac are studying, for after all, they must follow in their ancestors footsteps, the Vilna Gaon.

Back in my current time, Rifke sits beside me. She is not of my generation, and in fact is of my grandmother's generation. She feeds me chicken that she cooked for me, and she plays with my little baby. Through her I feel the love of my own Nana, long since departed, but never far from my heart. My own dear Nana who dyed her red hair until the day that she died. The day that I knew she had died because her spirit came to rest with me.

So many generations of women, apples of each other's eyes. Too afraid to say it, so you and I must name it.

Why is it left to us? Why we two in these disparate generations? But it has been left to us to name and tease out the stories, the pain, the love, the humor, the intelligence. This is what the story is in some part, a story of incredible intelligence. Intelligence, and love. Occasional confusion, but always a steadfast rootedness. It is up to us to explain why these many doors and windows into the past and the future beckon so strongly. In fact, it is for the very future in my hands, my small baby Odessa that I must write the stories that come before. It is for the very promise in my womb that I must put the stories down. The strength with which I feel my ancestors behind me, must be shared with those that come after.

It is like the beckoning colors of autumn, I must go as close as I can, weaving reds and oranges, yellows and the fading greens. I must inspect the brown drab leaves as well as the brilliant ones. This drive has always existed within me. There have been different periods of time in which I was able to investigate this, and somehow now, with Rifke by my side—this woman who shares my distant ancestry—I am able to begin again this investigation.

Again through another door, I see down the long line of broken, mismatched love into the recesses of the Lipton lineage. Different in many ways from that of the Gottlieb - Kartzinell, but there is a similar shared pain, a similar shared confusion all swirling around love.

We carry the weight of our ancestors on our shoulders, in our bellies, our hearts. It is an unspoken wordless dance. Yet we know, we know.

How many generations will it take to understand the cycles? How many times around the sun until we understand the burden and the delight? How much love will be gained and lost before we understand the real longing? What is the longing anyway? To fit in? To be a part of a family? To feel like me but at long, long last? We are a family that has had to leave our land. Yes, a long time ago so the scars are buried. But leave we had to do. There is no one left in the old land. Only ashes.

The continuity of lineage is in the crook of nose, the length of earlobe, the willingness to love. Yes there is the menorah, and the stories that go along with it. There is the shared catastrophe of the pogroms, and the Holocaust. But it is more personal than that which we must unpack and air out. The airing out of such stories will allow freshness, it's what will allow healing and peace to enter our shared stream. Somehow it is up to us.

Oh, there are many threads. Many threads that connect, many threads that are broken. Our tapestry is woven in both traditional colors and some that are more unusual. There are many lines to discover, many patches to inspect. This tapestry, this quilt is a complicated weaving, one for us to both pick apart, as well as remake. As a quilter and weaver, I know. It will not be easy. It will not always feel okay, but on the other hand it is a project which I have been working on all of my life.

When I was a small child I would ask again and again for stories from my Nana about her family of origin. How many times I asked her about her Zeyde and his red beard. How many times I asked her to tell me the story of how her family left Russia. And how long I dreamt of going back to that land. I knew all through my childhood that I would be the one to inherit the menorah. And when I finally did, I knew it was time to begin to think about traveling to its origin. In the journey that I finally took, I did not actually get to that place where the menorah was from.

But still I met ancestors, there on the river Dnieper. Still I felt them with me, in a present and very real way. "You did not need to come to our land to meet us," they said. "We were always here with you." Some might think this story has too much magic in it, too much surrealism to be real, but it is my experience. It is a real story and I have lived it. Where we come from so often determines where we are going. I want my little Odessa to be able to have answers to her questions, so I will do this work to make it so.

I stand up and I began to walk towards the door. I want to walk through, so I do. I walk through the door and feel the warm embrace of the Russian sun. And here it is already both simple and complex. For this is Belarus, this is Ukraine, but it was Russia. It was, in fact, the Pale of Russia. And it had been home to my family for many long years.

After cowering behind the embankment along the river while watching the pogram advance toward the shtetl at age 14, Merele (Mary) knew she was going to need to find a way out of Russia. Her two sisters had found their tickets to freedom—with men who were passionate Zionists, and therefore heading to Palestine. Her brothers were staying, staunch in their refusal to leave, but Merele needed a way out. There had been a young man, not much to look at, but with an occasional twinkle in his eye that she had noticed at the edge of the village from time to time. His name was Morris Gottlieb, he was the son of a woodcutting family. His family were not aristocratic like her own, and her parents would not be happy with the arrangement, but Merele needed an escape plan. She needed to be able to get out.

She formed an infatuation with this young man, and quickly he returned it as well. She was not in love, though maybe there was an amount of lust involved. Again, she needed a way out. She would wait for him by the river and shyly smile at him as he would walk by. He began to dream of her. And so when he finally asked her to walk with him one day she eagerly, if quietly, said yes. When he told her his family was starting to plan to travel to America, her heart began to race. Could she come too, she quietly asked? She began to dream about the faraway land where she would be able to walk down streets of gold, not hiding from the soldiers on their horses.

She began to dream of possibility, of music and freedom. She was a smart woman, having come from a family of intelligentsia, and so she held her cards close to her chest. After a few months of this quiet courtship, she gently told her mama Yehudit that she wanted to go to America. "The Gottliebs will take me with them," she said. Her mother, secretly distraught, was outwardly joyous for her daughter. Yehudit knew in her heart that her Merele needed this chance. Her other daughters already had their tickets to freedom, and she still would have her three sons close to home. Yehudit knew this would be a permanent farewell with her daughter, she knew she would not get to see her again in this life. She felt that she had been preparing for this moment all of her life, when she would have to say goodbye to this daughter.

She realized this was why she had been saving her own mother's mother's mother's menorah, keeping it safe from the soldiers, and holding onto it in a secret place.

This moment of leaving, "I'll say goodbye forever", has held me in thrall. I cannot conceive of saying goodbye to my daughter for a forever. I have never been able to imagine what this must have been like for Yehudit. This is the point in the story which I cycle back to you again and again. It doesn't help that I am now the keeper of the menorah. This object that ties me back to many generations of women. This menorah is a pivot point for me, a connector between me and my ancestors, tactile and potent. It always amazes me how much power this silver object has for me.

APRIL 2, 2016 – RIFKE

Dark but it is morning and you are communing with nature and I am recalling childhood in Washington Heights. Then Mildred married Aaron and in my then simplistic view of the world all's well. They moved to Yonkers. To me it was a leafy suburb of tranquility and joy like a Hallmark card. She gave up music and became a Mommy and taught sunday School in the Temple and Mary tagged along.

I do recall that Mildred liked Coach bags and I wanted to "hang out" in the Village and really we just visited - my mother, my brother, Kalman, and I. David ran around being himself. (I think he has changed less than anyone I have ever known) and really our paths diverged. I loved her but we didn't talk and I was a family appendage. Aaron started flirting with me and I treated it as big cousin stuff. I also was in a fantasy land because I knew all the European relatives were "somewhere else." That is, Sarah, they were dead in the villages of Bellarussia (as it was called.) Along with all those who stayed and stayed they were wiped out by Polish fascists and German soldiers. Aushwitz was in Poland.

Germany was to be free of Jews because we were unclean, disturbing, and generally pushy. I really grew up internalizing this view of Jews. I became protector of the Jewish voice but very tentatively. I did not join Hillel at New York University. I joined the leftist movement and knew Lorraine Hansberry and fell in love with a jazz musician and I held onto my little frightened self and my virginity. In short, I was without inner direction but was not self-destructive. I guess even then I had a self somewhere buried inside.

For several years we did not see Mary and Mildred and my mother was very hurt although she never expressed it. In the Jewish worldview, one never "talks" about feelings... All, is well. But it wasn't.

My mother, Yetta Papish, and my father, Aaron Pomeranz, who was Merele's cousin, were drawn to the Jewish Bundist movement, a survival movement and very anti-Czarist and hopeful of a human life for these shtetl youth. When it became impossible there, they wanted to come to America. My mother's ideal was Emma Goldman. My father wanted an education, but also much more. He loved music, poetry and enjoyment and he loved my mother. He was charming and she was serious. Merele loved Mildred and her hope was that she could promote her daughter's future, which was why she bought her a Steinway piano.

The marriage to Morris was non-existent as far as I could figure out from a child's perspective.

NOVEMBER 18, 2015 – SARAH

We are a lineage of strong women, yes. We sometimes drive away our men with our passion, our hunger, our need for life. *L'chaim!* We are the fiddlers on the roof, proclaiming our heart's song. We are the keepers of our flames, the Hanukkah candles burning all night long. We do not lose the threads, but rather weave them, continuously. There may be a gap in space and time while we get really busy - with music, with politics, with child-rearing - but we come back to the threads that inspire us, and we continue to weave, every free moment we get. This is part of what sets us apart. We do not waffle and waiver, we hold strong, and courage guides us.

We are romantic, believing that fairy tales come true, that they are the real story, that we can let them guide us.

One of my favorite stories about my Nana happened when she was a young girl. Merele, her mother, wanted the best for her little Mildred, her only surviving child. She spent years paying off a grand piano so that little red-haired Milly could take piano lessons - even when her father had to wait in a breadline for the weekly rations. Merele took her, walking the many blocks south into the City from their northern Manhattan building, all the way down to Carnegie Hall for the youth concerts with Leonard Bernstein. And, she would take her to the matinee musicals.

There was one such musical, Peter Pan, with possibly Jean Arthur as the star Peter, that they went to. During the scene in which Tinker Bell is dying, her light going out, Peter Pan pleads with the young audience to clap and clap so that their belief in Tinker Bell will bring her back to life. This little redhead goes racing down the aisle, unstoppable in her conviction shouting, "I believe! I believe! I believe!!!" 50 years later, or perhaps 60, my Nana is listening to the radio when an interview comes on with that very same actress Jean Arthur. The interviewer on NPR asks, "What is your favorite memory from your long acting career?" Jean describes that time she was playing Peter Pan and a little redhead came careening down the aisle towards the stage shouting, "I believe! I believe! I believe!"

I swear it was one of my Nana's proudest moments, hearing that story on the radio. The twinkle in her eye as she told me this story was so brilliant that I feel I have always been able to see the event unfolding as if I was right there with her.

Our romanticism is undaunted by "reality" and yet we still have a strong work ethic. If we want something, we work hard to make it happen. We fall in love and fall in love again, the truth is that our hearts are open, and we are faithful to that itself. Faithful to the love itself. And, speaking of love, it is strong and deep for our children. Things might not always work out. Yehudit, Merele's mother, had to say goodbye to her three daughters and Merele's first two children died. Mildred drove her sons away with her need for them, but the love remains a strong inner pulse. Part of my longing with my own daughter and possible future second child is to change some of the painful patterns, to not repeat the pain. This is my aspiration, and I hold strong and true to it.

NOVEMBER 19, 2015 – RIFKE

Thanks for being the keeper of our flame. I do feel even in old age that I was encouraged to be freer and more independent than Mildred. She was fearful of following her own road, her path. When she was finally "ready" to be her own person it was almost too late. She went to Maine to be near David (Sarah's father). He, of course, was searching for his own adulthood. You were this lovely young person thrust into the world and be an "other"—a Jew, a questioner, a traveller, a thinker, wanderer. You of all of us Jewish women listened to your own heart, your own voice, your own emerging sexuality. None of the women I know from the shtetl heard their own truths. Be good, love your cooking, or your family, or your beauty, or your jewels, or your things. Yourself? Pretend it exists.

NOVEMBER 20, 2015 – SARAH

Passion is sometimes blind, sometimes too driven and focused. Passion wants to control, as you say. And yes, letting go is the real love. I feel that I was the apple of my Nana's eye because she didn't own me, because though I was her only girl, I wasn't her child, and so that separation of time and space (she didn't provide me what I needed so I could take from her what was otherwise missing and she therefore had the opportunity to give it) allowed us to be true friends. It feels so similar with you, Rifke. You have the same driving passion, the same intellect and sharp wit, the same rounded and soft humor, but also the same sense of me as a person. How is it we lost one another for so many years? How is it we were able to find each other again?

Learning is something I feel our lineage has been passionate about. Does it stem all the way back to the Vilna Gaon? Do we feel that tingle and urge to read and write - as much as we possibly can? Because of him? Did I tell you that when I visited our distant cousins in Israel many years ago, I not only got to visit Yehudit's grave (a shock and surprise to learn she died one week after arriving to visit her two daughters and their families), but I saw a replica of the Vilna Gaon's synagogue in one of the large museums in Jerusalem. It was a pleasant shock to feel blood spanning so many centuries, to feel the same urge for learning and knowing.

Odessa, my beautiful daughter, is sleeping on my chest as I write. I stand at my kitchen counter, my gaze transfixed by the vivid blue of the sky. The sun has warmed me, the pain of learning keeps me sharp, and my longing to divulge more of the secret stories propels me to write.

I have no real answers, you know. I only have a dream sense of the family. After I visited Ukraine the first time, I contacted cousin Avinoam in Jerusalem to tell him that I had been back to "the old country." He wrote a scathing letter back, admonishing me for visiting that accursed place, saying he would never step foot back there. I felt bereft, I had wanted to share our common ancestry, to share the connection. I had stepped into the river, the river Dnieper, and I wanted to share the delight of that, to share the delight instead of what I had previously felt: the burden.

NOVEMBER 21, 2015 – RIFKE

Maybe all of us on my father's side had musical talent and we should acknowledge it. I love music and dancing, but after 4 years at Music and Art I felt that language (literature) and psychology were my strengths. Creativity takes many forms, as you know, and I loved being an English major. I did NYU in 3 years and read 10 hours a day in the summers.

I sat on our fire escape and immersed myself in romantic literature and in modern European literature. I teach from a psychological perspective and hold an interdisciplinary doctorate. I look at our background from Russia-Poland as a study in stamina and survival. Only a few of the relatives left and survived. Much of the emotional damage is expressed by the women-mothers in silence (depression) or in hidden shame and avoidance.

I find it amazing that close comrades like my mother and Merele could not trust each other enough to confide and find solace in mutual sharing. So what that Aaron betrayed Mildred. She became an even more vital mentsch after he left. She rediscovered her own self. She found her leadership qualities and became a teacher. It was not a "*shander*" (shameful act) to be hidden. It was a time she needed help and friendships, not victimization.

CHAPTER FIVE: RED AND PURPLE

All the people we love who have left us—they live inside our hearts, right here in our bodies, and they also sit on our shoulders. The colors we weave are red and purple—pain and delight. The tapestry is utterly both.

DECEMBER 15, 2015 – RIFKE

I think we also look at the men—Aaron, your grandfather, Aaron, my father who had Morris (your great-grandfather) in the rear of the drugstore nearly every evening after he was considered "persona non grata," by Merele (your great-grandmother). Your father, a man yes, or a *boychick* as that type of male was called and Jonathan who was more sophisticated, though that is also a thin veneer. Yes, the males so tortured first by ideology and then the victim role in Czarist Russia and the angry, controlling mamas. In the round belly that can be loved unfettered or loved distorted and mangled by frustration.

When I was in India in a safe house where Bill was the only male admitted and we two were the only Westerners, I was asked to participate in a woman's dance group as a therapeutic activity. I wrote and sang these words:

> *I Am a Woman*
> I am a self
> I will illuminate my world
> I will survive
> I will be strong
> I will prevail.
>
> I move gracefully with the music
> I close my eyes and dream
> I am young first
> I grow into my life
> I grow old.
>
> I am unafraid

Because I love myself
I love my friends
I reach toward the world
With joy.

I meet new people
Seek new adventures
Share laughter
Joy and even pain
With everyone
We share our dreams together

If I am shoved aside
I stand tall
Even if I am small
My size is measured
By my spirit
Even as we grow old
We together
Each alone
Are unafraid of the night.

I grow into my life
I grow old.
I will not simply survive

JANUARY 18, 2016 – SARAH

It is all real, and also immaterial. All the people we love who have left us—they live inside our hearts, right here in our bodies, and they also sit on our shoulders like *dralas* (the Tibetan description of helpful, magical beings) and they are also standing behind us, streaming out to each side like a diamond of wisdom and strength and support, the resource at our back. They are in the sunshine and the clouds, the wind and the water. The small, quiet buzzing of a fly and the large, impressive soaring of an eagle. They are in the laughter of children and the tears of elders. They are in the pain of memory and the delight of memory. They live within us, and we can bear them because they are our resource—not our burden. We can make offerings to their memory—setting out a cup of tea or vodka, asking them to guide and protect us. Our ancestors are our *dralas*, if we let them be.

JANUARY 27, 2016 – RIFKE

Staring at…Nothing
I used to see old women
Outside a building
Seated in the sun
Hardly moving
Seeming in thought

I never wondered
About their inner psyches
The threads of still life
Not ending their final days
Seated in wheelchairs
A blanket covering old,
withered legs

Did they love, or hate, or care
Or question, or beg, or sleep soundly
Dreaming of the future?
Of oblivion?
Frequently I noted
Their beautiful nails
Carefully coiffed hair usually blond
Did it please them?

I sit at kitchen table
As my mother sat
When unobserved
Blank, sluggish, immobile

To break this spell
I rise and pour coffee in a cup
It stands solitary and cold.

JANUARY 28, 2016 – SARAH

Thank you for this powerful poem. It struck me deeply. And, I remember so clearly those last months with Nana. It's why I returned from Europe when I did and why I waited to leave Maine again (which I longed to do then). I was with her nearly every day the last couple of months. Her humor was still in tact, but I'd catch her gazing out the window, wondering, dreaming, or just staring, perhaps. We often said, in my family, that her denial of her poor health kept her alive longer. I wonder if she was really in denial or just didn't want us to worry? I'm not sure.

I sure do miss her.

FEBRUARY 7, 2016 – RIFKE

So let's write...

I realize that we were politicized early in our lives as Jewish New Yorkers who believed in social issues as part of *Tikkun Olem*. Responsibility to those in need and not simply consuming for ourselves. Bernie Sanders is an example of this attitude and now we see the young (18 and up) responding to the one percent, how does that sit with you?

FEBRUARY 8, 2016 – SARAH

This is high on my mind these days, especially in the face of the choice between a woman as president or a gentleman who actually says the things I believe in. Early on, I realized I did not have the political drive that, strangely enough, both my mother and Nana had. Yes, those two women who did not like each other and did not seem to have anything in common actually both shared a very similar political drive. They both were very politically active throughout their whole lives. And I tried to be, when I was young, but it wasn't the right fit for me.

The notion of *Tikkun Olem* was not a spoken notion but nevertheless probably was and still is a driving force for my life. I am probably far more Jewish than I realize. A friend just told me that I write like a meandering Jewish song, repeating the chorus over and over again.

The choice between Hillary and Bernie for me is easy because I feel that Bernie is speaking the truth, without regard for what he will get out of it. Of course I long to see a woman president, but I don't feel that Hillary is speaking truth, not necessarily. I wonder so often what Milly would have thought - in the 90s she idolized Hillary and getting to meet her and shake her hand was a crowning moment for her in 1998. But I wonder, in the end, if she would have realized that Bernie was actually the one to vote for.

Tell me more about *Tikkun Olem*.

Help me understand myself and why these rivers and threads run through me so deeply.

FEBRUARY 9, 2016 – RIFKE

Sarah, the rivers and threads run through you because you really believe and you are not driven by ideology. Mildred was deeply unionized and her union (not ours, the college professors) was for Hillary.

The *Tikkun Olem* concept is what you did by going to Nepal and really caring about people, no broad slogans. I feel Bernie has human flaws but he really lives and believes that everyone needs health care...yes...every human being. I wish we were well enough to go to New Hampshire this week. I love you and am so fortunate you are my relative.

> The threads, rivers,
> Wheels
> Our symbols, our deep strain
> Hope for the future
> The nuclear plant at Indian Point, NY is leaking corrosive
> Deadly chemicals
> Drones are getting smaller
> Portable and deadlier
>
> The children drink from waters with lead
> Air is fetid and poisonous
> Why are we deluded and accepting
> Lies and slogans.
> Why?

FEBRUARY 11, 2016 – SARAH

This is where my Buddhist practice and path come in: I choose to see that life is much, much more than just the slime and muck. Of course life includes all of that, but it is up to us to rise above it, just as the lotus rises to the surface of the muddy pond and blooms gorgeously for all to see.

Life is what we make of it. If we are stuck and think it is only muck and mire, then that is what we will see. If we remember to feel our hearts and look out and up, we see the brilliance of the sun, we feel the vastness of the sky, we connect to possibility and beauty and love. This, I feel, is the ultimate *Tikkun Olem*. Because when we live from this place of brilliance, it automatically communicates to everyone around us - we can become the stone thrown in the water that creates the ripples that spread compassion. Or, we can become the stone that thrown in the water sends up cascading waterfalls of mud. It's up to us, really.

So our own delusion is simply that, a construct of our minds. It is completely possible for us to cut through our own confusion and rise up a bigger, wiser being - which we are already.

I think Mildred saw this in me, and nurtured it. Then I found the Shambhala path that helped me to articulate it. I feel so ridiculously fortunate.

FEBRUARY 12, 2016 – RIFKE

Yes...we must rise above the muck and excrement but we must also recognize it and try to eradicate it, I believe. If not we will have horrible bigots and manipulators and as Holden Caulfield said, "phonies."

You radiate love. One feels it and we respond.

How are you feeling? Pregnancy going well? House holding up with Odessa getting more active and moving around? News!?

FEBRUARY 18, 2016 – SARAH

You caught on, I've been sick all week with a tummy bug. Finally better today, feeling much more normal again. The pregnancy seems to be going fine, regardless. I meet with my midwife next week for the first appointment. I just can't believe I'm 8 weeks pregnant and there's a little kidney bean in my belly again. It's really throwing me for a loop. And you did this 3 times!?

The house looks like a one year old lives here, which is actually quite delightful. Her favorite things are to hide balls under the cabinet, take out all the Tupperware from the cabinet, and push around her wagon (and climb into it). She's snoozing on the couch right now so I'm getting some work done. I'll write more ancestrally soon.

FEBRUARY 23, 2016 – SARAH

It seems I may be miscarrying right now. We are resting in sadness and uncertainty and have to wait another week for the health insurance to kick in before we can get an ultrasound.

Thankfully we love each other and have such a bundle of joy in Odessa. Please send good wishes, it is a heartbreaking moment. I'm not telling very many people at all until I know more.

Sending love and gratitude for our connection.

FEBRUARY 23, 2016 – RIFKE

Dearest Mammelle Sarah: Bill and I ARE HERE WITH ALL THE LOVE WE HAVE...

FEBRUARY 26, 2016 – SARAH

It was a miscarriage.

RIFKE
Wish we were with you.

MARCH 2, 2016 – RIFKE

Never
My daughter said once again
Write of your childhood
That tiny apartment
An oriental rug
Antique wing chair
A magnificent
umbrella stand
And a piano
Refugees crowded our carved couch
I never knew who'd be in our living room.

A displaced professor from Warsaw
A musician who fled the Nazis
But had his metronome
I cannot speak of their pain
Family found in the rubble
Of scorched earth
Holocaust remains

A culture destroyed
A language lost as Latin
How did it all begin?

Never my father told me
Write propaganda
Empty, shallow words
I remain silent
I cannot explore this grief
I am not worthy of the voices
Of the perished

So "never" remain my theme

I write of new
Palpitating horror
My world waging wars

Plunder. murder, torture
We scorch another people
A different group
Not my people.

I scream at night
The sweat, the ache
The knowing
The bodies

Carried away

People waving fists
at us
Never, I said.
Never is now.

MARCH 3, 2016 – SARAH

You. Are. So. Powerful.

This poem leaves me stunned and reminded that there are so many of us. So many of us who love and live and never know. So many of us who never not-know too.

Our society does not know how to relate with loss. Loss is scary. We don't like to feel it and we don't like to proclaim it, partly because we know nobody else knows how to deal with it either.

I had a miscarriage last week.

There is just about no one who knows how to relate with a miscarriage. It is not comfortable, it's terribly sad and our society just doesn't talk about it. The sadness stays hidden, brushed under the rug until it becomes a huge, silent elephant sitting in the corner of the room. The families who lose the potential new being become isolated in sadness, and if they are lucky find some way to celebrate or make an offering of their sadness. I did not have the option of burying anything and so my offering is the following letter.

Dear Departed One,

You had such a tiny chance. You grew for only such a short time in my belly. It was such a short while to be your host and I felt that something was not quite right. This was not because I rejected you, no, I welcomed you and would have relished the opportunity to bloom with your growing, go through labor and birth you and spend the remainder of my life loving, nurturing and celebrating you. I would have cherished becoming your mother.

But something or some combination of things intervened and you were not to be, not to become. I feel that you ceased to become even before you had the chance for sentience. Perhaps, somehow, whoever you were to be decided now was not the right moment and I was not the right host.

I am both bereft and relieved. It cannot be one or the other. I am bereft of the honor and opportunity of loving you, and I am relieved that since you were not to be, I am unburdened.

What is it like for you? You who still float in transition, neither here nor there, nor anywhere in between. I do not believe who you could have been had already coalesced. There was no specific body that was evacuated from my body. You had not yet emerged as distinct, and so I do not mourn the loss of you so much as the loss of the potential of you. Whoever you were meant to be may yet still become. Or, the potential of you may linger closely tucked next to my heart for the remainder of my days as the unfulfilled promise of blooming. And I will long for the promise of you.

I will work to feel proud of my discerning body that made the choice my heart never could have. I will work to trust the wisdom of my body and to trust that one day I will bring another to fruition. But you, whoever you would have been will always live inside of my broken heart.

Your loving mother, Sarah

What I wish to shout from rooftops for all to hear is this: In the face of great loss, may you find the courage and the heart to be with it, to reside in the midst of the uncertainty and pain. May you trust your body's wisdom and let the grief move through you in the waves that it naturally moves in.

Red is the color of my sadness. Red is the color of my broken heart. Red is the color of my unfulfilled longing.

MARCH 3, 2016 – RIFKE

Purple is my color of age and loss and sadness. But it is also my color of hope, of defiance, of life. Bill and I are your beloved and we grieve with you and Scott. We are with you both. Sarah, I have loved you from afar since you were a lovely child. Please accept our love…You taught me to accept yours. O.K.?

MARCH 28, 2016 – SARAH

Time moves on and I am on one of my subbing shifts at the local food co-op. I'm a manager there and get to work once, maybe twice a week in the evenings. It's a big store, all delicious organic and healthy stuff. The store is slow, I've already helped a couple of customers find what they were looking for, and I've checked in with all the departments.

I am in the beverage isle, fronting and facing, pulling forward the coconut juice. I close my eyes for a moment, listening to the whirr of the fans, the distant hum of the music in the dish pit, the laughter of a small girl in the produce section. And before I know it, my mind has swirled back in time.

There is a swelling of pride as I feel the cool touch of can to hand. Strangely, I belong here, shuffling cans and bottles, arranging boxes on shelves. Surprisingly, this is part of my heritage. On both sides of my family, my ancestors owned grocery stores. On my mother's side, there was the great Magoon Grocery Company in Littleton, NH located right where the ugly Bank of New Hampshire now sits.

On my father's side, there was Lipton's Market, a grocery store in Fleischmanns, NY that my great-grandfather Sam ran. I wonder if his ancestors had a store in Dniepopetrovsk, Ukraine (what used to be Ekaterinaslav)? But even older than that, even before then, my great-great grandparents Abraham and Jehudit Karzinell (Jehudit who was descended from the great Vilna Gaon) ran a dry-goods store in Pinsk, in the Pale of Russia, what is current day, Belarus. I wonder, did they start this store, or inherit it? Perhaps from Abraham's family, since Jehudit's family were talmudic scholars.

It is to this oldest store that my mind often runs to when I get caught in the delightful monotony of fronting and facing grocery items. How many generations ago did we start selling goods? Does this answer my continual love and longing for the old-timey market? As I have traveled the world, I have collected stories and memories of markets, from old New England farmer's markets, to the original market in New Brunswick, Canada to Mexican street stalls, Nepali markets rife with odors and sounds, to Thai fish markets, to Dutch flower markets, and many, many more.

I am always drawn to the conversations that happen in these places of trade. Drawn like a moth to the flame to see the fresh produce, to feel the soft skin of a peach, to smell the rich aroma of fresh ground spices, my mind instantly imagining the long journey of that peach from tree to stall, the spinning tale of seed and sun and water and human intervention.

Whose stories lie tangled in the one journey of an orange? Whose tale is intermixed with the lone flight of a seed from vine to wine bottle? How many lives have touched this spectacular red pepper? Who grew the cotton and wove the cloth and died these gorgeous pinks and oranges? And what is the story of this simple shopkeeper who sells me this stunning sari?

I long to know, did Jehudit die her own cloth? Did she drip her own candles? Did she sew her own clothes to sell? Did she make the hats that inspired her daughter to encourage her husband to become a milliner in New York, in the new country? Was it through this store that she obtained the menorah that she gave to her daughter when she fled for the streets of gold? Or is it as I suspect, and long to know, that the menorah was her mother's mother's mother's?

You can see why I like to work at a grocery store. In some strange sense, it is a home-coming for me. There are other aspects of it I like of course, I am a manager and so get to float and be responsible. I like that, it serves me well. But more than that, besides the ancestral connections of it, there's the community aspect. And this too makes me think back to all of my grandfathers and grandmothers throughout the generations and lineages that owned and operated stores, for this enabled all of them to be that spider at the center of the web.

Historically, markets are the center of a community. Wherever there is food and water and wine and cloth, there is life. Therefore, whoever has the goods to offer is the giver of life, and can therefore be trusted with secrets and stories and gossip. Communities gather around this hub of life and activity. And we, we of my lineages, love that. We love being at the center, holding the reins of the stories that swirl around us. Merchants. We get a bad rap, but we have held the fabric of society together. We weave society together because we hold all the strings.

I re-open my eyes, there is a page for the MOD, which is me. I drop the story for the moment, but know that I will forever continue to come back to this thread of continuity.

RIFKE
What is good about your store is that it is a cooperative not a personally owned store where the proprietor seems wealthier than the people who shop. I am basically a socialist, I think, and drawn to Bernie's philosophy. The Jews in Poland-Russia could not work the land and became "Handlers" (sellers of goods they could not raise) because they had no land. They had a few cows or goats if they could afford them. The poor fled to the *"goldeneh medina"* a mythic land of milk, honey and oranges. They never even saw peaches!

CHAPTER SIX: WHO IS BEHIND THE WOODPILE?

The question "who am I?" never goes away. We turn to ancestors, we turn to the unanswered questions, we turn to one another, and in the quiet rushing sounds of an oncoming storm, we hear a semblance of an answer. Again and again, we can ask: who is behind the woodpile? And every time, come up with a more potent answer.

APRIL 2, 2016 – SARAH

You are less than a mile away and I can't get *Tumbalalaika* out of my mind! I sang my daughter to sleep with it. And it didn't take long, she went down like a flash!

There is so much in me that is answered by you. The questions that rise up in me are answered by your frankness, your purple hair, your stories of the war years. I have spent my whole life wanting to *know*. Longing to feel what it felt like to lose so many. The horror seeping in with the howling of the wind. There is such a part of me that wants to have been there, to have seen it, to have felt it and smelled it and tasted it.

What was it like when they lined up our ancestors and shot them, one by one?

What was it like when their cousins and friends and neighbors were marched beyond exhaustion and made to take a "shower?"

What was it like to look back at your daughter and in that split second moment understand you would never see her again?

What would they think of us now for having German friends and driving German automobiles?

I crave your Yiddish. It rocks me to my bones. I have never been able to adequately explain my connection to cultural Jewishness, or my unquenchable thirst for stories from The War. There is nobody in my immediate family that gets it or feels it too. I often have explained it to myself by feeling that I *was* there, in a past life. That I was a Jew who escaped over the sound from Denmark to Sweden, but all of my family died. I felt that when I crossed the sound from Alborg, Denmark to Malmo, Sweden in 1999. I felt that I had been there before, and I knew it to be true. I was 19, and everything was true then. But somehow, this explanation still hasn't left me.

It doesn't really matter why, but the haunting connection is still there. And in you, I find an embodiment of what I crave. The language, the songs, the stories, the lived, cultural memory. You embody what I long to remember myself, and can't.

We have to eke out every ounce of this connection while we can. I love you so much, and am thrilled you are here for the weekend!

APRIL 3, 2016 – WRITING NEXT TO EACH OTHER

SARAH

The Lamed Vovnick—the ordinary person found in the millions of people, a symbol of the guy with broken down shoes who has the biggest vision.

Investigating the threads and tendrils of connection and intersection, the shards of clarity and pain and love. Memories swirl, stories unite but the question always comes down to: why me? (Such a Jewish question, *nu*?) The incongruity, that I am a Jewish gal, longing to know the stories, thirst quenched with Yiddish. *Tumbalaika* fills my whole mind as I walk down the road.

Brushing off the cobwebs of desire, I suppose I must admit to the thread of questioning. Of course the story is about me, and of course I don't want it to be. I am shy of owning this particular passion, of admitting this particular inheritance. But that's just a story I tell myself because nobody else (besides you) can see it.

If the truth is to be told, I must own this story. I must show up and be as present to this, for the sake of absolving my sad and downtrodden (and sometimes strangely successful) ancestors, as well as for the sake of coalescing an inheritance to pass on to my children. Because that is also part of the truth, that I feel poised between the rich support of ancestors unseen, poised to become a funnel for truth and beauty and love and also pain. My children will receive a true inheritance, and if they are lucky, won't have to dig as hard as I have had to understand it and know it.

I don't want to be a schmuck, and that's probably why it's hard for me to own the story. I am the lowly tuba player at the back of the orchestra, I am not the illustrious trumpeter with the loud solos. It is my role to support others in blossoming.

But in order to do so, I must give these ancestors their voices back. This is part of the vision that I hold: that I am a keeper of my ancestors voices. If I get quiet enough, I can hear them. And if I look carefully enough, I can see them in the reflection of your eyes. In some kind of way, the "why" question of their lives is answered in us, here and now.

The power and depth and passion that has spurred me to question all my life, which has sent me careening thousands of miles across the planet to walk on the streets that they walked, is answered when I feel this thread of time. Continuity hums like a cello in perfect tune.

The *lamed vovnick*, the one who secretly holds vision. This is probably us, my dear Rifke. This is probably us.

The particulars of the stories don't really matter to me—who slept with whom and so on. It is the thread of love and passion and vision that inspires me. It is the power of that passion that drives me. It is this question of inheritance, received and now to be given that calls me to write.

Of course I want to write some of the particulars, the how and why of Merele leaving Pinsk. My own personal phenomena of the menorah, the light that it brings to my life, illuminating connection and inspiration. I hold vision, and that is the position I am entering in the course of my recent entrepreneurial career. So perhaps that is why it is *right now* that we have come again together to the same table to hash out the wheres and whys and whats of our story and shared ancestry.

The fact is, Rifkele, there is nobody else in my family I can go there with. Nana was the last one for me, my father won't go there, my uncle can't stomach it, and my brother is only interested in my findings, not the journey itself. It has been a lonesome 17 years since my Milly died. I am sure that I was not ready until now to plumb these depths with you, but I am also sad that we lost all that time. Oye, regrets in this department will not help. I am grateful we are here, at last.

The tonic of this writing goes deep for me. I feel it in the way the wind blows in these pre-spring trees. I feel it whirling through my dreams when I sleep. Knowing my place in the world has taken a long time, it was never all that obvious to me, probably because my parents—in their own intricately different ways—never knew *their* own places in the world. There has always been clarity for me as to who I am, but it was always only metaphorical, and therefore deeply secret. I am the light-bearer, the beacon, the visionary. But who can say these things out loud without being laughed out of the room? But Nana saw, she knew.

So yes, I will own this story. But I want to know what your part is too. Is it that we have these threads of blood that connect and through connection there is reflection? Is this why red wine appeals to our conversations? We find the lines of red and trace them together? Women, mothers, lost babies, we live and love and grieve. We can weep and we can guffaw, coarse and fine, deep and sublime, political and psychological. But somewhere in the mix, a shtetl, a river, a woodpile to hide behind.

"295…I can't count any higher," you told me she said. Our forebears needed not to talk about it, they knew. But I hunger, I yearn, I need to talk about it. I need to describe the woodpile Merele hid behind when the pogram came to town. I need to speak the names of her brothers and their families who were lost with all of your parent's families. I need to plumb your memory for the scents of shtetl life that I am too many generations removed from. This yearning will drive me bananas if I can't give voice to it. There I go again, wanting to shed the light.

I have none of the answers, except for the whispers I can detect in the wind and the catch in your voice. Shedding the light means for me an arousal of courage: I must go where my family doesn't want me to go. When I told my Israeli cousin Avinoam that I had gone back to where our ancestors were from, he condemned me for returning to that blood-soaked land. I regret that it was our last communication, he who had been so generous to me when I visited Israel in 2005.

But living into my skin, inhabiting fully who I am, means *I am this too.* And so, perhaps, here in my 36th year, my daughter over a year old, it is time for me to proclaim this. I will try to stop explaining it and just get down to business. But isn't this style of apology also my inherited Jewishness?

This fire is almost as if Merele, or further back, Jehudit is sitting on my shoulder saying into my ear, "Come on already, get down to business, just proclaim who you are!" And this too feels like a thread. Who, in our lineage of women, was fearless enough to proclaim themselves? You just sat there across the table from me telling me how my great-grandmother and my grandmother both lived lives they thought others wanted them to live. Neither found true happiness or satisfaction, you seemed to say. Both of them tried to live through their children to relieve and satisfy them, and we both know that isn't the best path to take.

You must know by now that I'm in the business of being genuine. This is my version of meat and potatoes, and I am in fact, hoping to make that a real equation, that being genuine will provide for my family. So this is the time to ask these questions, to taste these flavors and give voice to these themes.

It is not for the outcome, other than the inspiration to have something to share with my own children and perhaps great-great grandchildren, but it is the process. To grow deeper into myself as a visionary, I must know all the parts. So it is, yes, it is, a personal investigation to liberate this hidden Jewishness within myself.

Who is behind the woodpile?

RIFKE
How can I write in a more urgent tone? Our *Yiddishkeit* is rapidly disappearing because we are disappearing—as a people, as a culture, as a voice from the diaspora, as a very bleak moment in human history. The Holy Wars, the flights to yet another place, Spain, France, England, Greece and so on to the 20th century and the

attempt at the final solution. Great philosophers like Heidegger and Spear pronounced the importance of racial cleansing like an emotional high colonic.

Yet we are here in bits and pieces and remembrance of things past and we find each other and love each other and search for each other and are unstoppable and very eager to learn about ourselves and our history and it does reside in ourselves—not out there from a great visionary. We need to remember that we did not emerge from a nowhere place. Like Allen Ginsberg's *Howl* we are not madmen but we cannot be voiceless, and so we write on tablets, on paper, at desks and tables and in places we have arrived at as wanderers.

Sarah, you are a woman from this past. You have a menorah; you had a village in the swampland (the Blotehs) and you are a singer like the great cantors and like Moshe Oiysher and Shalom Aleichem, and pieces of women's writing from medieval England as your babies were destroyed in the blood libel horror. There is Bob Dylan (of changed name) singing of loss "where have all the flowers gone" and I sought you out because I love your difference, your belief in the focus of presence, your child sharing your dream, your great writing, and your teaching other women of many other cultures to open their own visions and flower as you have.

We are perhaps queer, whatever connotations that signifies. There are no borders and no boundaries in our expressiveness. We have breasts and also parts unknown even to our brother Chagall who flew over the ghetto, away from pogroms and ended up a Jew in the US. Wasn't he French or better yet Parisian? No, he was an international Jew always in flight over garrets and churches and manmade instruments of torture.

So we sit and write. I, old, wrinkled, sipping red wine, amazed at this quiet spot in Vermont. Our partners are themselves, not our agents of goodness, but they support us because we need it. Our empowerment is in our need. There is our Jewish thread. Never too self-concealed, other-directed, or fearful of expressing that need for love. I, myself, write from a sense of longing, of desire for escape, of need for greatness and of finally hope my self-knowledge will say, "Cut the shit and be near people like Sarah who say I can darn your sweater. I can know your pain. I will be there when you need me. Will you be there as well?"

"The Past is the present. Isn't it? It's the future, too. We all try to lie out of that, but life won't let us."
~ Mary Tyrone in Long day's Journey into Night by Eugene O'Neil

>Bleak day in London. Going to see where Karl Marx sat in British Museum
>He choose my kin in the villages of Pinsker gubernya
>To spark their escape from the misery of ghetto life
>Insulated from the world
>Yet isolated from a vision
>Of hope.
>My young mother
>Not yet mine
>Her dearest friends
>Running, reaching, hoping, questing
>It is here in the new World
>We found each other
>Old now, you young mother
>The heart continues its search.

"There is no sub without a shadow, and it is essential to know the night."
~ Albert Camus, *The Myth of Sisyphus*

Well, Sarah, I think our families knew much about the night. There was never enough laughter growing up. Everything was ultra serious. That certainly affected how Mildred and I were raised. Nothing of frivolity entered the door. Were we ever childlike or childish? Thoughts running through my mind this morning. That loss was palpable and guilt was the undercurrent of every action.

OCTOBER 20, 2017 – RIFKE

I do know about love and death. We go on or drift away like martinets pretending to function and to stay in touch and always try to smile. But then a word, a note, a call comes through and it is from you, Sarah, and that makes all the difference, as Robert Frost wrote in *The Road Not Taken*… "Why?"

I have known many young women with sweet words and sweet faces and kind hearts. So many entering and leaving and some stopping to sip some tea or wine before the goodbyes. Why Sarah? It cannot be blood or family. I do not love that way. So why does my heart race when I think of this specific Sarah?

Then it comes to me…an epiphany, a revelation, an understanding. We are connected as Jews, parts of the deep suffering through thousands of years, through long marches, and escapes from tyranny. We meet across generations and search for ourselves in each other and our friendship prevails. Even after years of not communicating we pick up and rejoin each others spirit, heart, deep understanding. Yes…there is a Jewish connection. So we must always tell our stories to each other and to all who share our vision.

OCTOBER 24, 2017 – SARAH

I think there is a rugged genuineness that connects us. I do think it is grounded in our ancestral roots of Jewishness. There is a no-holds-barred, genuine fearlessness and joyful honesty to our communication. It stretches beyond death, as I feel I can taste our ancestors in the bittersweet liquor of our conversation. I get a taste and I want MORE.

I remember standing on the hilltop in Dnepropetrovsk, Ukraine, the city that used to be Ekaterinaslav, the place where all the Lipshitz came from, not your lineage, but half of my Jewish heritage. There was a modernist statue of Catherine the Great on that hilltop, as it was a city that had been named for her by her illicit lover Potemkin. From that hilltop, I could look out and down and see the bend in the river Dnieper. Flowing through that same water is the water from the river that goes through the shtetls outside of Pinsk, where our ancestors were from. I could feel the grandeur, the *passion* of a people sentenced to live by other's laws but longing to be free to live their own way. I could sense our ancestors clustered around me in that moment, celebrating my freedom, celebrating my strength and ability to walk forward by knowing what came before.

You embody this rugged genuineness for me, just the way my beloved Nana Mildred did. You *see* me. And I see you. And we don't have to explain or make up stories about anything. This is an enormous gift in an age when things are either hidden or over-explained.

We don't hide behind fear, we acknowledge it, and therefore move through it. I feel in another life we could have been sisters.

I agree so deeply with what you say, and I want you to continue and respond to me and I will respond to you, and this will keep the threads moving forward, just as through the river Dnieper our ancestral waters flow into the Black Sea and eventually up into the clouds that then bring us rain here in New England.

OCTOBER 24, 2017 – RIFKE

There is something else we have in common with Mildred. We never set out to prove we are superior to... anyone. We try to embrace and to unite and to protect and to seek ways to find solutions and give us hope. It is a love of life and a real joy in being alive. Klezmer music embodies these qualities and all three of us share this love.

We are intelligent and we know that politics is always human manipulation but.... as Jews we do know that we do not know.... We question, we search, we cogitate and we always retain our sense of humor and our love of those we really know. Do we know? Yes, we do know how difficult living is and how painful loss is and we know when we encounter the "real deal or the real person." You are my younger voice, my spirit that says, "You may falter and stumble but you will never crawl or victimize the other." That is my view of our present era and my younger voice.

NOVEMBER 7, 2017 – SARAH

Sometimes that intelligent cogitation leads to more suffering. Sometimes the pain is so vivid and real that the weight of carrying it means I must look back to my ancestors who carried that pain before me to remember that this too is my inheritance and I can do it.

Seeing what is real, that actually seems to be the burden, the pain, but also the mysterious gift and delight. I ponder this as I have stepped onto the path of motherhood myself. How I see what is real and how I carry that and pass that on - this seems to be the most important. Getting caught up in the busyness of daily life, well, that is one thing, but the other thing is reconnecting every day to the reality of life - the realness of life, the realness of being alive. This is what I see in my daughters eyes when they look back at my eyes. That beauty, that spark, that realness, that is what I live for.

That spark is, in fact, the magnificent truth of what I love the most about life. It is what I crave and seek. It is what I hope to inspire others through all of the work I engage in and create. That spark is where you and I meet - you, perhaps my older voice. If I am your younger voice, you are my older voice. For somehow, we speak the same language.

So the spark chases the spark and ignites awareness of the true flames that light the way for others. We will not victimize anyone else, we will wear the badges of our own courage like the red flag of dawn on this November day. And again and again and again, remembering the truth - the truth of freedom, of love, of living truly in the midst of the chaos of the world creating itself around us day by day.

FEBRUARY 2, 2018 – RIFKE

I sit
It is easy
That's a truth.

I feel
An inner pull
"Contact Sarah"
My heart says

She knows
She understands
She is your link
To the present.

She is also
Your past
You loved her
Jewish grandma

Who really cares
Or knows.
We both share
Beyond language.

FEBRUARY 5, 2018 – SARAH

Your words pierce my heart. So, here is a response:

    I sit.
    It is easy
    To look out and taste the view.

    White hills cascade to the distant mountains
    Odessa is 3 today
    Indigo is 7 months and
    almost crawling.

    Raven soars by, black against blue
    three years ago
    I was birthing

    And every moment
    I am birthing
    churning from within
    the foamy froth
    of my inner life

    Leadership
    is the bread and butter
    but
    Love
    is
    the guiding hand
    that spreads the butter.

    I lean in and the metaphors
    of snow blowing in wind
    rip
    at
    the garnet strings

of my heart.

I feel you sitting beside me
my Rifkele
my Nana's favorite young cousin

What it is to share this
is
the best
of the best.

FEBRUARY 6, 2018 – RIFKE, SARAH

RIFKE

There is no reason
Under sun, sky or earth
Anywhere
Wonder, question, analyze
There is simply no reason
To love and to hope

There is no reason at all
That's reason enough
It is without meaning
In the wind and chaos
It is you.

SARAH

In the blue
and gray
of sky
I see

no, feel
I feel the wind
and taste
our blood

Our blood
that whispers
secrets
and stories

The stories
that unravel
my truth
your truth

Our truth

And that is
the intersection

Hearts beat
booming
blooming
unearthing
dark tendrils of secrets

Those secrets
that were once
proclaimed
and hidden

Those secrets
that bare the truth
and hold nothing back.

P.S. It is only with you that poetry comes these days. Poetry that is sustenance.

RIFKE

We know
Hidden, volcanic hurt
Anger subdued in
Brilliance and achievement

We know
The buried treasure
In arms reaching
Embracing

The insatiable need
To find that comfort
In shared love
Needed as sustenance

You have discovered
That tiny kernel
The drop of nectar
The soothing delicacy

Wordless, soundless
Bolts of brightness
Affirmation, acceptance.

FEBRUARY 15, 2018 – RIFKE

Desire
I never believed in wishbones
Or their power to signal life
Or serve as a distraction

My wish bone
Lies on the cutting board
A talisman
To slice or remove

Detritus, dirt, dissolution
There it lies
Waiting - trusting - thinking
Of the void
Ahead.

FEBRUARY 19, 2018 – SARAH

Earth
Bones rising up
from cold earth
embrace my sad and wizened heart
death comes without warning
and so we get to live
each day
we breathe

Dissolving into the air
each breath
gives rise
to each
sparkle
of sunshine
and warmth
and love

Trusting
this dance
is the only
way
forward.

CHAPTER SEVEN: ACCESSIBLE DARKNESS

When we lean in like this, bearing with the process of discovery, we find that the obscuration of darkness transforms instead into a pathway towards the light.

FEBRUARY 28, 2018 – WRITING NEXT TO EACH OTHER

SARAH
Sitting together at your home. Girls are asleep, mostly. So we talk and drink peppermint tea and write together.

What binds and connects us? It's not just that we are cousins. It's not just that my grandmother was your cousin.

It's that *realness*. It's that straight from the gutness. The darkness is accessible. There is no need to cover it over or explain it away or prove anything differently.

What is the connection? Love. Realness. No bullshit. *Being seen*. No need to explain, there is a sense of already knowing. Like a tree that tastes the dirt around it's roots, it already knows the flavor. Sure, it may shift with the rains, but there is a recognizableness.

These layers of correspondence are like peeling the layers of fruit to get to the core pit at the center.

No, really. What is this?

How else to say it, but that when we sit together, you and I, Rifkele, I can feel all the women of our lineage convening into this one presence. This one sense of joy and suffering, of love and longing, of connection, belonging, and pain, all mixed and swirled together. We become the melting pot. We become the stew cooked for hours over the hearth fire. Our flavors blending and mixing, but ultimately nourishing and maybe even sometimes delicious.

It's in these moments of remembering, memory beyond myself, reaching far back into reaches of time I don't even understand, and yet feel, taste, skin prickling with the extra sense of it, it's in these moments of memory that I feel reborn again, able to take flight, because my feet are truly and deeply and irrepressibly rooted in the real soil of my origins.

Origin story. Perhaps that's what this is all about. Hasn't humanity had an obsession with origin story since the beginning? Going back to the origin. Original. Organic organs of evolution. Where do we come from? What is our beginning? It is beyond our own mothers and fathers. Our origin lies within the tangled webs of our ancestors. And when there is this glimpse of ancestry remembered inside of me, there is this hearth fire, these babushkas, these homemade candles and picked apart chicken. There is red wine and tears, there is blood and death and birth all mixed together. There is fire and life and truth.

When I taste this, I feel fully alive.

When I felt my Nana's gaze, your Milly, I felt fully seen.

When I write with you, Rifkele, I know the truest story. The layers have fallen open and the truth is laid bare. I am. And that is.

In this being, in this becoming, in this already fully fledged burgeoning, there is a sense of completeness understood. Nothing more longed for, other than to continue, to perpetuate and to gift this experience to others. To you. To my daughters. To their children. And so, I write in hopes of cracking open a sliver of that possibility of experience—for them. Not for me, because this is already known to me, no I write so that I might shine that light of remembering this moment for my future unborn descendants. If this is even possible, I do not know, but it is and has always been for them that I write.

I am, therefore, in my truest self and realest sense of human, that bridge, that shining light that I always have known myself to be. I shine the light on what *is* so that you too, might see and *know*. This is my role, my job, and possibly my inheritance. Though as we have spoken of, this inheritance has been latent in recent generations. Perhaps it was my great-great grandmother Yehudit who saw me in the future, and for that, passed along the menorah so that when I saw it, I too would know and remember.

Perhaps this whole thing is a conversation I am having with her, with Yehudit. And for whom—yes, for my great-great grandchild. Perhaps this is a communication through the ages, and I am simply a conduit, a "carrier" of memory. And so, I must capture this experience, it is not only imperative, but it is my birthright. This is the curriculum I must pass on: how to sink into the remembrance of beings past, and pass that forward through generations to come. That is continuity, *tantra*, in Buddhist terms. And in this, I am the teacher passing this transmission along.

What exactly is the transmission then? It is to stop, feel, and look inside into that place where you taste your blood. It is that place where you go beyond your own birth, back further than the time in your mother's womb, back even before your mother was in her mother's womb, and back even before that to a time and place you can only imagine and dream about. Bring that dreaming forward and look over your left shoulder. There, you can see her, your great-great grandmother is a child, and she is being instructed by her mother in how to make candles, drip, drip, dripping by the fire. The hot wax stinging her young fingers, building calluses that will harden as she ages and bears her own children singing into the world.

Now close your eyes. Take a deep breath and notice what you smell. The scent of our ancestors is right here with us, we take them with us wherever we go. "We have never left you, you were never alone. We have been here with you all along." Clustered around you, and propelling you from behind, they are there, they have always been there, and they have been waiting for you to see them.

I, your ancestor, dear reader, am also here with you now. I and I and I, we are all a part of you. In this way, at least, you are never alone.

This goes beyond politics. Beyond spectacular jewelry and coach bags. This goes beyond the silly songs and stories of childhood, back to a place of origin. Where meaning makes sense and senses are overridden by memory, memory of this very moment. In this way, there is nowhere else to be. Anything else is a side-step of where we actually are.

Correspondence with the moment, that's what this turns into. For memory becomes present. The gift that goes deeper the more you stay with it.

So, Rifkele, let's please turn this into a gift for others. Please. Let's do this.

MARCH 2, 2018 – RIFKE

Some words: Truth, honesty, acceptance of flaws....This is for me the totality of life. We are daughters of revolution. Who were the landowners with slaves who wanted power of their own?

The Yiddish tradition was one of pain, ghetto life in the shtetl, or planned escape. The entire Polish-Russian community of over six million perished in gas chambers and starvation camps and with it a language and a culture. Revolution? Hardly.

We are here. Parts of the withered wish bone and the self-denial. I have two wishbones now lying on my cutting board. They are nearly cracked, fragile, waiting to be thrown away as pure garbage. Are we broken? Are we whole? Is there a link between your resilient spirit and my old nearly extinct gaps of survival?

I want to believe "yes" but that is an illusion, a mirage of illusion. I want to believe our table talks are profound and our shared phone chats will rock the world. Is it an arrogant illusion? We will discover the answers together by doing it and experiencing it and knowing what the answer, yes, the truth really is. This is not a sermon on the mount or any other expression of dogma. Just us reaching, touching, loving.

MARCH 8, 2018 – RIFKE

OUR CONNECTION

I cannot think of visiting a museum or even the site of the violence and pretense that went along with the murders of over six million humans in Poland and Austria and France and Germany and…As I write to you Poland has declared they were not "responsible."

How can they even think about what was done and dare to pass legislation proclaiming "innocence?" Our relatives were buried alive in the villages where they had lived amid non-Jews in supposed neighborliness and friendship.

What is that insane dream alive in Wagnerian opera of whiteness or blue eyes or height or muscle or physical power that six million people had to die for? They were gassed, desexed, buried alive, for what purpose? What is our present society like? Have we become a loving, peaceful human environment that looks at death sites as if it no longer exists? What is our present? How have we changed? Do we love more, change our thinking so that it never occurs anywhere and certainly not in Poland or in the United States? I can't bear to be so hypocritical that I join a "tour" and walk around a death camp rather than confront myself where I am. What are we fostering here in our own lives? I wonder…

Yes… I have been thinking about our connection. It is closely tied to our Jewish spirituality. You do not ever seem to be Christian (whatever that represents in our global society). You are warm and soft and passionate and intense. I see these as ethnic qualities. I feel you understand me without my needing to explain all of life's symbols. I am also so impressed by how you love and relate to Odessa. She knows she can count on you to nurture her loving qualities and teach her not to use Indigo to vent frustrations. Great you both could play on the rug after she returned to the house. Beautiful to be part of it all. So wish we lived closer and I could be that extra pair of hands in tight moments.

MARCH 16, 2018 – RIFKE

Lost Words
I lose some at night
Precision or incision?
The cut is in my heart
Loss of children
Hunters not hunting.

Rifles mow down people
Not tall grass
I reach toward your giggle
To hold and hug you.
I do not lose this
Moment together.

MARCH 20, 2018 – RIFKE

Have written about childhood too many times. I don't recall any longer having a childhood. I was supposed to be grown-up. I cried a lot but "cry baby" grew up in whatever mangled condition and had a life. And now? Age, wisdom, dignity, self-knowledge. Of course not... Age signifies loss. "Be careful. Don't climb there. Don't lose your balance. Don't fall." Should I be balanced? Should I be a model of rectitude and correct behavior and moderation?

Should I? May I? Can I? Loss is a daily occurrence...of love, of touch, of passion. Why pretend? Do we know each other? Do we know ourselves? Do we feel the grasp of another under water preventing us from oblivion? The dark moon envelops us. Everything, nothing, silence, cracked empty shells on the beach. Waves come in and pull us out. Waiting... Submission.

APRIL 30, 2018 – RIFKE

Long Division /Ruminations
The quixotic titles
Of arithmetic structure
Short/Long division
It has been long
Bizarre and endless
Leading to more breaks in the road
Hills, rubble, twists, and deep ruptures
Always divided
By endless endings
Silence and confusion
Clashing weapons and fiery feuds
Capulets, Montagues
Blue eyes, bleached bones
Beached whales
Mountains to climb
Disappearing in mist,
  heat and frozen limbs

  Still here?
Why, I wonder
But one question I do not question
Or expect a response
I smile, I wonder
When it happens
It will be long time coming
Swift conclusion.

MARCH 2, 2018 – RIFKE

Free Fall
Are we connected in free fall?
Do we create from castoffs?
Jewelry, shapely artifacts
Design and color
We idealize our bodies
We need to believe
What might that be?

Knowledge
Imagination
Hope
Dreams?
A cataclysmic voyage
Ours…ours
Until we cease.

JUNE 5, 2018 – RIFKE, SARAH

RIFKE

> *Words*
> I teach language to utter what words
> Never say.
> Endings…choice…thought
>
> My student sits at table
> Near me.
> She sips herbal tea
> I do coffee
>
> Wake up?
> Alert?
> Cream thickness
>
> Do I believe we make sense?
> I teach five words, I say
> Equality, choice, feminist, philosophy
> Forgot fifth word
> Reality?
>
> Too overwhelmed with grief
> Of self
> Silence… fifth word?

SARAH

the silence of birdsong
springtime dirt
bubbles in response to
needed rain

making sense
of earth
solves the riddle
in my heart

the silence of birdsong
trills and thrills
soothing
the ache
for ancestors

the dirt is
our bloodline
the mud
remembers

and we rise
we rise
sunshine
is the song
in my heart

CHAPTER EIGHT: CONCLUSION, FOR NOW

Clearly, this correspondence has been a dance. It feels timely and timeless all at the same moment. We circle back to close this for now, knowing there is so much more to come, knowing that it is not perfect, but that perfection was never the point.

MARCH 8, 2020 – SARAH, RIFKE

SARAH
Astounded that the journey has come galloping to this precipice of sustaining awareness.

So many years of writing, living, unearthing. So many threads woven: let's be honest, there is irritation in dissonance, we survive among shards, listen to our ancestors, dance in red and purple, repeatedly ask: who is behind the woodpile? Through our investigation, the darkness becomes accessible, and we come to some kind of conclusion, for now.

To a large degree, I have trusted this ancestral dance.

I have savored the slow reveal.

I've always been a sponge. I got the message from a super-early age that since I was emotionally savvy, it was up to me to help heal and fix everyone around me.

I learned that if I try to take on what someone else is feeling, I can help them feel better. For a while.

This played out in my family when my parents went through a messy divorce and at sixteen I was the one to pick up every single piece.

This played out with my school friends every single day on the bus or in the playground. They'd come to me with their problems, their complaints, their troubles, and I'd advise and counsel them.

Of course I gravitated to youth ministry work when the opportunity revealed itself. Of course I ran the show when Nana died. Of course I made all the pilgrimages to the ancestral land. Of course I dashed to visit my dying great uncle Harold a few days ago, though the pilgrimage took on epic proportions due to already being sleep deprived from a trip across the country, and my dead Grandpa Aaron took the wheel and steered me south instead of north for two hours on my already lengthy way home...

The thread that connects my intersections is *pain*.

I spent so much of my life optimistically seeing possibility that I didn't even recognize the pain I was pickling in.

Until recently, I didn't even acknowledge the taste of anxiety, even though I now know that the flavor has been familiar for a long, long time.

I inherited a lot of pain.

Not physical pain, exactly. But I used to call myself a "heartbreak specialist" to my friends, who would come to me in droves with breakups, deaths, and challenging transitions.

Fortunately for me, and for them, and for you, I recognized that I needed more information, more training, more understanding.

If I am to truly be of benefit and help another human being navigate pain, I realized, I need to understand it myself.

So I dove down the long slippery slide of Buddhism head-first.

There were many layers to my twenty-plus years of training. Probably the first layer was the dance of familiarity. Just gaining clarity about what a path actually is, how to practice meditation, why it's important to do so, and what the overall path looks like. This beginner's stage was full of excitement and challenge and discovery. The discovery tasted a lot like coming home to myself for the first time. The challenge smelled like encountering dirty laundry you thought was clean but really needs to be hand-scrubbed. The excitement was the slow reveal of possibility that unfurls when you unclench your fist and discover a pristine little cherry blossom tucked up inside.

I accomplished this first stage of the journey through my tenure at Naropa University and in my study-abroad program in Nepal.

Losing my mother the following year and then living in Nepal again seasoned me into readiness for the intermediate stage of my journey, which happened during my five years living in Boston.

At that stage, I dove in so thoroughly that my entire universe was Shambhala—I cooked, ate, drank, slept and sang every fiber of my life through the teachings and in the community. And I grew mistaken about some of the messages I was receiving.

I kept hearing a familiar restrain from childhood friends who had pushed me away, even though I was so busy "helping" them, that I was *too much*. That I had to restrain my tears, pull back my excitement, let go of ambition.

I received the memo that the journey itself is about polishing away the impurities of craving, wiping away the blemishes of passion, steam-ironing flat the creases of aggression, and shaking out the cobwebs of sleepiness.

Every moment is an opportunity to be *AWAKE!*

Now, from my perch on the other side of "advanced practitioner," I see how both brilliant and painful those teachings are. They are brilliant because they are true— we can't wake up to ourselves without becoming familiar with the habitual patterns that hold us back. But they are painful because if you begin to believe you are supposed to be...anything other than you already are, you've missed the mark.

The true inheritance of these mind-heart-teachings, is that we already are exactly who we need to be. We don't need to change or fix or bend or break. But we do need to be gentle with ourselves. We do need to remember to take care of ourselves as we slowly open.

For me, the "advanced" stage of my journey incorporated incredibly challenging lessons of patience. And in the end, it turned out there was nothing to wait for.

Now that I'm on the "other side" of the last twenty years of my life, and my community has fallen apart and the direct access to teachings have seeped away, I am left with my own devices. My own deep ancestral journey has brought me here. And I couldn't have stumbled my way here without this deep investigative writing journey with my beloved Rifkele, now perched upon her own brink near the end of her life.

I can see how from an early age I *knew* pain. I could feel it anytime someone near me banged a toe or scraped a knee. I could feel it in the tension between my parents. I was drawn to it, too. How many times did I bear witness as an animal lay dying? The bleating sheep on the Welsh moorland, the choking pelican on the Santa Cruz pier, the freezing kitten in the back shed, the goldfinch spluttering on the roadside after flying into my windshield. The worms we buried in a cemetery in second grade...

I remember my first real human-death. Randy Bean. My first boss. Look him up—he was a jazz legend in Maine in the early 90's. I remember savoring the stabbing ache in my heart as I sobbed and sobbed and sobbed. I was 14.

It was only a year later that I started to lose people in earnest. Grammie, whom I never really got to know. Grandpa, whom I longed for desperately but who never knew how to connect. One of the greatest fortunes of my life was Grandpa's younger brother, my great uncle Harold—the very same now on his deathbed at age 94 who I just visited two days ago—he knows how to connect, and almost every time I've ever seen him, we cry together about how much we love each other...

It was Nana's death that took me the next step in learning pain. Nana, my Nana. My beloved Milly. Rejected by the rest of the family as too needy, too clingy, too, too, too, she and I clung together. She saw me. She witnessed me. And in her eyes, I bloomed. The apple rose of her heart.

I knew the moment she died. And I took care of everything having to do with her death. I was only 19.

These many deaths, others not named, friends who tragically died too young, friend's mothers who flamed out too early, they all prepared me to be able to walk my own mother, estranged from me until then, towards her death.

And later, I showed up to walk my beloved mother-in-law towards her death.

It's not that I never knew how to feel pain. It's not that I didn't understand pain. I was just so wrapped up in it. I knew how to *celebrate* pain. And that certainly was true in my two birthing experiences.

It was this understanding that the human condition is inevitably intertwined with pain that drove me to the Buddhist path.

Many long years of meditation and introspection, deep *dharmic* reflection, and training honed my ability to bear with the poignancy of pain.

If we don't sit with it, we can't learn from it.

If we merely push it away or try to cover it up or excuse it or fix it or change it or ignore it or buy more stuff to camouflage it or put makeup over it or duct tape it or a fake plastered smile it, we will gain no altitude on our experience.

But if we decide, right now, on this very spot, in this very moment, to change our allegiance to let ourselves actually *feel* whatever we are feeling, we will allow ourselves the opportunity to tread carefully into the depths.

We don't have to go it alone. There are many, many friends along the way. And that's who I have patiently sculpted myself into being.

The tapestry I have been busily weaving these many years is the multi-hued quilt that can keep you warm as you sit on that windy cliff pondering your own mind.

I was so steeped in pain, and much of it not my own, that the deepest part of me knew I needed to step onto a path that could teach me how to tease apart what was mine and what was other's. I needed the pause, the gap, the space to see clearly into myself because I had been so cluttered with the stories of everyone else around me.

My emancipation from the specificity of the journey, due to a #metoo collapse, has allowed me to step onto my own windy precipice and look back and *know*. I know who I am. I know that I'm a beacon. I know that my job is simply to shine, shine, shine.

And I know how to create and organize systems that will magnetize and benefit multitudes.

By putting myself first, finally, I have learned how much more I have to offer.

I will drive up and over all the mountains to see you before you die just so I can tell you how much I love you. And I will allow the pain to rebirth me into a more weary, but more fulfilled version of myself, more ready than ever to dig my heels into the spring mud and spring forward into shining the light on your journey to the great, wide world of *awake*.

The conclusion, for now, is that the songs of our ancestors will never stop singing inside of me. The conclusion, for now, is that I am indebted with gratitude for having been allowed to ride these waves of memory with you. The conclusion, for now, is that I wish for my daughters to someday learn your stories and be further enriched by them.

The conclusion, for now, is that our song will never stop singing in this wide, wide world. The truth is that this exploration has brought me home to myself in the truest possible way.

RIFKE
The love of shared feelings and direction of lives crossing mountains of words and denial of the obvious is part of the human condition, I think.

Death is the underlying fear that guides our searches for the perfect foods to eat, the correct exercise to engage in, the best way to celebrate that we are stumbling north or south for years searching for that special road, that great healer, that perfect spiritual label until it is obvious it is right there all the time. The market hidden messages tell us how to look, how to address the lonely crowd across the chasm but we don't really need any of it.

We could simply try what Sarah and I have been doing for years.

It is to tell each other how we do really connect as ancestors and as two woman very old and one getting there through going to Nepal and just about everywhere. It is here.

I loved her Mildred and she loved her Sarah and we three are enmeshed in each other's continued search through our Jewish paths, our love of lovely fabrics to wear, and our wandering around the human globe.

We offer some of our ways of connecting in joy and in frustration. It is Holden's searching for Phoebe in Central Park in that huge city by the river…Manhattan, says poet Whitman.

All we have is love baby…do we know the answers. They are right inside of us until we are rendered voiceless.

And so we offer some of us to you and hope you also find the persons in your heart waiting to hold you close.

It is simply love.

AFTERWORD

SARAH

More than five years have gone by since we began this epic journey of discovery. More than twenty years have gone by since I lost my Nana. A decade has gone by since I first set foot upon the ancestral homeland in Ukraine. I have birthed two babies, lost one, launched two businesses and written numerous books. I have grown garlic for four seasons, and traveled to be with Rifke numerous times. Though she is perched upon the precipice of the final life transition, her spirit is strong and our bond remains unbreakable.

I could not have found the strength for this investigation without the steadfast love and support of my husband and partner Scott Robbins. I would not have known how to dance with the dragons of mind if it were not for the Ukrainian sister companionship of Ella Reznikova. I would have been deeply alone at heart if not for my aunty Deborah Lurin. All of my other friends and family members who have remained by my side through all the thick and thin, I would name each and every one of you, but I don't want to leave any of you out.

All ancestors are by our side, when we let them. They rest deep inside of our hearts, providing the warmth at our backs.

May these words be of benefit! May all beings remember to look back and truly *see*!

May it all be so!

ACKNOWLEDGEMENTS

We could not have accomplished this deep work without, first and foremost, the support of our husbands: William Krummel and Scott Robbins. They not only gave us room at various dining tables, but baked cookies, served chicken dinners, and refilled our wine glasses many times, and moreover gave us the space for our connection to blossom.

Getting this work to a point of publishing required the support of a number of incredible colleagues. For a kind editorial eye and heart, thank you to Paula Diaco (https://writestoriesnow.com/). For innumerable read-throughs, layout support and design and many, many hours of supportive conversation, thank you to the inimitable Lee Purcell (https://lee-purcell.com/): we could never have made it to the finish line without you.

For website design, support, collaboration and brilliance, thank you to Jim Infantino (https://slabmedia.com/). For perpetual belief in our work, exhaustive conversation and devoted friendship, thank you to Shawn Shouldice McShane (https://www.shouldicemcshane.com/): I would never have believed I could hit the publish button without your support!

This work is dedicated to all who come after us and want to look back in order to live forward. To my daughters Odessa Rose and Indigo Poppy, I hereby bequeath to you: the blessings of your ancestors.

Learn more about Sarah Lipton's work at: www.sarahlipton.com

To read more from Regina Krummel see: https://www.goodreads.com/book/show/4383379-looking-good

ABOUT THE AUTHORS

Regina (Rifke) Krummel
Regina received her Ed.D from Columbia's Teachers' College, taught at NYU, Columbia and many other universities and schools. She retired from Queens College CUNY, after 33 years, as Full Professor, Emerita. She has spent many years doing poetry therapy and creative writing in prisons in the UK and USA. She trained future high school teachers at Rikers Island's male prison. She did poetry therapy in the New York State women's maximum security prison in the psychiatric division of the institution and published a book of their poetry, and a book of her own poetry: *On the Ledge*. She continues to teach creative writing in an adult program in Connecticut. Together with her husband Dr. William Krummel, she has volunteered in India and China in the area of education and professional development for teachers of English. She believes living is an endless search in expanding one's knowledge of the world through teaching and exploring new cultures, including the dehumanizing effects of the whitewashed American prison system.

Sarah Lipton
Sarah's passion for travel, contemplative practice and writing began when she was a small child in Maine, gazing longingly at the ocean, and the imagined worlds beyond. So she traveled internationally before going to Naropa University. Since then, over the last two decades, Sarah has guided thousands of leaders as they navigate the creation of thriving cultures. Through her business, *The Presence Point* (pending B Corp certification) Sarah works with organizations longing to empower their leaders from the inside-out. Her passion is rooted in over twenty years of service, contemplative training and teaching in the Shambhala Buddhist community and stems from the conviction that when leaders are genuine, society can bloom. She is also the founder of **GENUINE, Inc**, a 501(c)3 nonprofit organization that focuses on transforming society through community. Sarah is a keynote speaker, podcaster, visionary and author who now lives high on a hill in rural Vermont with her husband and two small daughters. Learn more about her here: www.sarahlipton.com

www.ingramcontent.com/pod-product-compliance
Lightning Source LLC
Chambersburg PA
CBHW051407290426
44108CB00015B/2182